ALL THAT TWITTERS IS NOT GOLDBERG

ALSO BY THE AUTHOR

So So Wisdom: The Misplaced Teachings of So So Gai

Mixed Emotions

Wordapodia: Volume One
An Encyclopedia of Real Fake Words

For more information on all writings, projects, and public appearances —past, present, and future— please contact matt@tipofthegoldberg.com or call 856.796.0610

ALL THAT TWITTERS IS NOT GOLDBERG

TRUTHFUL HUMOR FROM A VINDICATED COLUMNIST

MATTHEW J. GOLDBERG
AUTHOR OF *WORDAPODIA, VOLUME ONE*

iUniverse, Inc.
New York Bloomington

All That Twitters Is Not Goldberg
Truthful Humor from a Vindicated Columnist

iUniverse books may be ordered through booksellers or by contacting:

iUniverse
1663 Liberty Drive
Bloomington, IN 47403
www.iuniverse.com
1-800-Authors (1-800-288-4677)

ISBN: 978-1-4502-6395-5 (pbk)
ISBN: 978-1-4502-6396-2 (ebk)

Printed in the United States of America

iUniverse rev. date: 11/4/10

Especially for BJG
Benjamin Jun Goldberg
(For now, *Baby Ben)*
You are growing more beautiful
And more fascinating
All the time
Thank you, my son, for all the thrills
You give me and Ruby every day
(One day you'll read this and say, "Huh?")

Contents

Acknowledgments

Initially, I'd like to thank SPG, RJG, BJG, and TXQ.

SPG—Sara Passo Goldberg, my mother of loving memory. Your sense of humor, encouragement, and love are still great sources of inspiration and comfort.

RJG—Robert Joseph Goldberg. Dad, you continue to be a lifelong learner. You were/are a journalist in the true sense of the word, a great friend and as terrific a father as I could have hoped for.

BJG—Benjamin Jun Goldberg. Benny, it is indescribable how much joy you bring to all you encounter. Continue to grow and never lose that sense of joy—along with your inquisitiveness and your love of everyone and everything around you.

TXQ—Tan Xiao Qian, or Ruby. Thank you for putting up with all my, um, idiosyncrasies. I'm thrilled that we're taking these journeys together.

I'd also like to thank Dahris M. Clair, who publishes *The Infinite Writer*, the e-zine that took me on as an almost-anything-goes columnist in July 2007. Yours is a labor of love, and I appreciate everything you overcome every day to write and to lend a hand to fellow authors.

Thanks to the following people—and I may be forgetting some—who read several of my columns "hot off the press," and offered feedback: my dad, Robert J. Goldberg (always a terrific writer and journalist); my brother, Josh Goldberg; former roommate and great friend, Dave Gelfand; tennis bud and friend, Neal Slutsky; and my Toastmasters International colleague (and writer), Akweli Parker.

Speaking of Toastmasters, I credit that organization (with a shout out to my Voorhees, New Jersey, club) for *forcing* me to come up with material for speeches, some of which paved the way for my columns (and vice versa).

For all those I have unintentionally snubbed and those who unbeknownst to me have read my column faithfully online in addition to all those who are about to enter my world, thank you for finding something of value—whether it is insight, humor, or something else that resonates with you—in my writings.

So enjoy, and as my *mohel* no doubt expressed on that fateful day, I hope this is merely the *Tip* of the Goldberg. Please stay tuned.

Preface

Responding to the call for *a columnist to write for a new e-zine*, (an electronic magazine; I wasn't sure what it was, either) I submitted two columns of random length and waited to hear if I had been chosen at the right price—at least from the publisher's perspective. I was and have held a spot in *The Infinite Writer* since July 2007 that I have titled "The Tip of the Goldberg."

Though unpaid, it's a fun and somewhat rewarding gig and I usually take to the keyboard on the last night before deadline, usually meeting it, and usually writing something that I've been told has some value.

The beauty of writing an almost-anything-goes column like this is that I can choose the topics that I write about. Sometimes, I write topically from a current events standpoint (the 2008 election, or my Philadelphia Phillies on the brink of winning their second ever World Championship in 126 mostly futile campaigns), or maybe it's seasonal (*resolutionary* ideas for the New Year), or perhaps it's an event in my own life (anticipating my first foray into fatherhood).

In all cases, I hope that the columns stand the test of time—if only a brief amount of time, cosmically speaking—and point out universal truths, observations, and humor that we all can relate to.

In terms of tone, because I like to write in what I call "real time," you get almost an unfiltered sense of what I'm thinking ... sorry about that ... and my voice tends to be irreverent (but not sarcastic), open-minded (I hope), and a strange brew of naiveté and jadedness. I hope that I come across as a humorist in the best sense of the term, and I hope that I earn your laughter and even your tears—or almost tear-inspired *farklempt-ness.*

Above all else, enjoy, and if you're moved to share any thoughts, ideas, or feedback, my contact information can be found within.

2007

One-on-One Interview

July 2007

This is the initial (remote) interview I gave for The Infinite Writer e-zine, replying to questions from editor, Dahris H Clair.

MATTHEW J. GOLDBERG, author of *the unintended collector's items, So So Wisdom: The Misplaced Teachings of So So Gai,* and *Mixed Emotions: Poetry for the Open-Minded* is here at last. Without further ado, we'll jump right in.

Editor: Hello Matt—we finally meet face-to-face, in a manner of speaking. Before we begin the interview, I'd like to thank you for offering to write a column for our fledgling e-zine.

Matt: My pleasure.

Editor: I believe it will also be ours after reading some of your work. At some point, we'd like to use the Collingswood story, as I'm certain it will resonate with all our writers out there. I enjoy your humor, as I'm sure they will, so welcome aboard. First question: Tell us about your previous works. Have you won any awards?

Matt: I have been writing in some fashion for many years, but thus far, I have only had two books published—*So So Wisdom* and *Mixed Emotions*. But over the years, I have produced a strange cornucopia of poems, comedy routines, and other writings, including several musical comedies for kids and senior groups. Along with ghost writing a variety of humor pieces, I have in recent years written a children's manuscript and a play/screenplay that I hope to refine and publish soon. I am not aware of any awards that I have won for my writing, but I don't always check my mail.

Editor: You began to write poetry as a student in the second grade. Did you realize at that age that you would want to write in the future? What was your dream for your life when you were in elementary school?

Matt: Well, one of the pleasures of publishing *Mixed Emotions* as a POD book is that it allowed me to include some of my poems from second and third grade; like my dear mom of blessed memory, I am a pack rat and my wife and I still trip over boxes of my yellowed keepsakes. I always enjoyed creative writing, but as an eight-year-old, I recall being consumed with more worldly concerns like achieving world peace and not getting beat up on the school bus. Other than that, I had vague dreams of becoming either a major league ballplayer (my hopes were dashed when I was cut from the high school baseball team) or a lawyer (it would've required actually attending more than 42 percent of my college classes).

Editor: To what influence do you attribute your penchant for writing satire?

Matt: That is a great question for which I, unfortunately, do not have an equally effective answer. I suppose that I have always had a very irreverent sense of humor, both in day-to-day life and as a writer. As a somewhat creative thinker, I see humor in many situations and I try not to be a slave to convention and pretension. I also try not to detach myself from situations in a sarcastic way. There are few writers who do satire well, and I don't know if I am among them.

Editor: Judging by what we editors at *The Infinite Writer* believe, the reading/writing public has a real treat in store. Tell me, what authors do you most admire and why?

Matt: My short list would have to make room for Maya Angelou. Her *I Know Why the Caged Bird Sings* is my favorite autobiography, and I also love much of her poetry. Not only is she a gifted writer, but one senses her humanity, her indomitable spirit and her zest for life and for justice in almost everything she writes.

Other writers that come to mind for me are Mark Twain—a marvelous storyteller, a great wit, and someone who transcends time and place. Also, Harper Lee, if only for *To Kill a Mockingbird*. What a courageous, important book that is told with such honesty, passion, and compassion in a very unique voice.

As a movie buff, I'd also like to mention my favorite screenwriter, Paddy Chayefsky, who authored original screenplays for *Marty* (incredibly touching human drama), along with *The Hospital*, and *Network*, the latter two being brilliant satires that resonate and inform more than thirty years later.

Editor: I agree. Those are memorable contributions. You are a teacher of Hebrew. Does your talent for satire creep into your teaching? Or does your livelihood influence your writing? If so, please tell us how.

Matt: I have taught religious school—as a side income if you want to call it that—for more than fifteen years. And I never would've predicted doing so, as most of my memories of Hebrew school are of sitting in class waiting to be rescued early, so I could jet off to a youth baseball or basketball game. I'm not sure how teaching (I have taught in other settings as well) has influenced my writing, but I would say that my sense of humor has been important in getting me and my students through some boring and trying times in the classroom. And I am the type of teacher who gets taken aback by a quiet room; I like to shake things up or even be the class clown from the front of the room if things get too staid.

Editor: In your acknowledgments you say, "This book would not have happened without my wife, Ruby." How did Ruby influence your writing? Is she the reason you chose a Chinese philosopher, however irreverent, as the protagonist, or to put it more aptly, the sole character of your book?

Matt: Nah, I just said that to make her feel good. So So Gai is a fictitious nineteenth-century philosopher who was a womanizer, overeater, games hustler, and all-around swell guy. He has become an alter ego (or is it altered ego?) of sorts, and in many ways, I think he symbolizes how I envision Ruby pictures me. Does that make sense?

Anyway, on the surface, Ruby is from mainland China, and uses the expression "so-so" to describe a lot of people, experiences, and things. It was also during a trip to China that I, during an extended bout of insomnia, communed with my fictitious altered ego, and wrote about three hundred sayings, some of which found their way into my book. But I also attribute my ability to take some time off from "real work" and publish a book or two to Ruby's patience and generosity.

Editor: Although your individual style of humor is reflected in your poetry, some of your poems are quite profound and stimulate the mind of the reader. Is that why you chose to title it *Mixed Emotions*?

Matt: In part, yes. My poems span a variety of years, emotions, and styles of writing. I think that it took me a long time to find a poetic voice that was not too humorous or too wrist-slashingly serious. So I think that many of my poems embody the dualities and complexities that even us so-so guys have. But also, as I write about in the Introduction, I have mixed feelings about poetry itself. In a nutshell, I love poetry for the freedom of self-expression it affords the writer and the reader, yet I loathe so much poetry that I read because it can be so arcane, pretentious, or self-indulgent.

Editor: What plans do you have for additional works? Are you working on anything at present? (Besides your August column of *The Infinite Writer.*)

Matt: First of all, I am delighted to be a part of *The Infinite Writer* and hope to contribute something of value or at least something of amusement. I am working on revising *So So Wisdom* to make myself more of a character, if you will, and to update the philosophy to make it more modern and universal. My other projects include the pursuit of a writing style that will lend itself to regular newspaper or magazine columns, and the revision of my children's book that will serve as somewhat of a memorial to Lucky—the most lovable cocker spaniel the world has ever known.

Editor: A man after my own heart. I identify with losing your heart to a blessed little animal. Well, Matt, I have enjoyed this conversation, which has told our readers a lot about the man, the philosopher, and the writer. We'll all be anticipating your column as a breath of fresh air. Thank you for giving us some of your precious time.

Matt: I thank you for listening.

Editor: And there you have it, folks, straight from the so-so horse's so-so mouth. As we say in the newspaper business, "Let's put it to bed." See you next month.

Guest Services

August 2007

Atrocities against our beautiful language are being committed constantly by people and entities that should know better—teachers, writers, television talking heads, and newspapers, to name just a few. Inundated by such abuse, I decided to not only take *inaction* (by limiting my own sometimes felonious writing) but to also take action against one of the biggest culprits out there: the neighborhood supermarket.

When did the Customer Service counter at my local Shop Rite become *Guest Services*? Maybe it happened one day three or so years ago when I was joyfully comparison-shopping for bug spray. And perhaps it happened on the same day that *Customer Service* moved permanently overseas. I remember taking notice of this development one day when I ran through a torrential downpour to purchase my weekly bagels.

While groping and caressing six dark sesame bagels with the plastic tongs (I am a considerate customer), I looked over to see the *Guest Services* sign. I was excited to see the sign; as a guest, I was looking forward to a nice cup of coffee and a warm towel to dry my drenched, overweight self. Little did I know that Maggie at *Guest Services* would offer me neither of the above, although she pointed out that there were some beach towels on sale in aisle 13. My earnest protest that they should treat their guests a little better fell on her deaf, dry ears.

Ever since that incident, I have secretly seethed whenever I have seen a *Guest Services* sign in an inappropriate venue, namely one in which I was at least potentially a paying customer. Nobody has seen my outrage, and no *host* at a supermarket or bookstore has ever been asked for a warm towel, a glass of lemonade, or even a tour of the master bathroom. But I want you to know that I have been silently bristling and my tacit acceptance of this language abuse has bothered me no end.

I have pictured myself as a combination of Kramer or George (Cosmo Costanza?) in a *Seinfeld* episode, discussing this with Jerry. "So, my truly good, if sarcastic, host asks me, 'With global warming, poverty, and hunger in the world, you bristle at the sloppy and devious abuse of language perpetrated by our nation's grocers?"

"Oh yeah," I reply. "I bristle. Better believe it, buddy, I bristle."

But what's the use of bristling when I can do something about it? In a recent conversation with myself, I decided that if the Shop Rites of the world were going to consider me a "guest," then I would make sure that they lived up to their end of the bargain as good hosts. My mission to strike a blow for language lovers and abused customers alike would require that I trade in my jaded worldview and cynicism for a façade of complete trust and innocence. In preparing for this mission, I might even have to play dumb. My inner voice told me that this wouldn't be so hard to achieve. My inner ear didn't know how to take this.

My quest for truth, justice, and a satisfying shopping experience took me to a Shop Rite about fifteen miles away from my home. As I untangled one of the shopping carts, I couldn't help but whistle the Disney "Be Our Guest" song, something I had never done before. While still humming the tune to myself, I approached *Guest Services* with an air of entitlement mixed with humility.

"Can I help you?" asked the almost-pretty Alex from behind the counter.

Before answering her question, I decided to be a good guest by not reminding her that *cans* are displayed in aisle 17, but yes, she *may* help me.

"Yes, you may," I answered in my most pleasant guest voice. "First of all, I wanted to compliment you on your name tag. That's very considerate of you, Alex. But do you have any name tags for us guests so that we can identify one another while we're staying here?" My hostess smiled the half-smile of the slightly perplexed and didn't answer. Should I have said *we guests*?

"Well, maybe you can help me," I continued. Do you have one of those sheets that identify this week's specials? I thought I would save the special items for the other customers."

As a considerate guest, I thought it only fair not to assume I was any more special than the others who were staying at Shop Rite. I straightened the camera case around my neck and resumed my query. "And also, I'll be staying here for quite a while. I noticed that there are no beds for your guests, and I hate to impose on you further but being from out of town, I wondered if you could recommend any inexpensive motels in the area where I might get a cheap rate for one or two hours?"

Now wearing the exasperated look of the totally bewildered, poor Alex responded in the best way she could. “We’re all out of circulars, but I think there are some next to produce. May I help the next guest?”

I suppressed my urge to snap a picture of her and pushed my cart along toward the produce aisle. My goal was to fill my medium-sized cart with enough nonspecial items of every variety. So, as to fully enjoy my stay, I thought that I would also grab a bite or two from the nice spread that my hosts had prepared. I also sought to engage in a conversation or two with some of the other guests.

Noticing an attractive brunette weighing her plums on the scale, I peeled a banana and offered her half, allowing that it was unusually good. Looking slightly amused, she declined before wheeling her way toward the cheese shop. Slightly disappointed, I left half of a banana on top of the banana cluster for another guest who might also not want to overeat.

While selecting a nice bottle of olive oil, I learned that the middle-aged man who was comparing the ingredients of a few jars of bread crumbs lived just a mile away, but grew up in Italy. When I asked him if the Italian grocery stores treated their guests so well, he stared at me as if I had a third nostril. Perhaps it was because I had a few stains on my shirt from the Buffalo wings I had sampled.

Feeling a little thirsty, I worked my way over to the orange juice. Picking out a generic brand of low-pulp OJ, I started to drink from it until I remembered what my Mom had told me about drinking from the carton. I grabbed one of the Styrofoam cups from my cart and poured myself a nice cup before returning the container to its refrigerated shelf. I then opened a package of Post-It notes and took a pen from my pocket. I affixed a note on the side of the carton that said, "Very refreshing. Thank you, Alex and family."

I wasn't sure, but a crowd of guests seemed to be watching me as I wheeled my way around Shop Rite, noshing some potato chips and filling my cart with a prudent assortment of meat, pasta, paper goods, and household items. When I paused in aisle 15 to brush my teeth, there appeared to be quite a few more guests and hosts watching me. I nodded shyly to one or two, not wanting to open up a one-sided conversation.

With my cart almost full and hoping to not overstay my welcome in any way, I knew what I needed to do. I picked up a nice bouquet of flowers, and took out a thank-you card from the pack I had selected. While waiting for the other guests to leave Alex's counter, I had enough time to add a personal touch to my card, and to also enjoy my slice of pumpernickel and apple butter. Waiting for just the right moment, I handed her the pink carnations and then followed with my little card.

Apparently left speechless by my largesse, I thought that I would speak first. "Alex, I did not want to embarrass you, but I just wanted to show some of my appreciation for a most enjoyable stay here. If I'm ever in the area ag—"

"Excuse me, um, Matt," a more experienced hostess interrupted, while staring at the name tag I had discovered in the school and office supplies aisle. "You are not allowed to open up packages and move other items around in this store."

"Oh, I wasn't aware of that," I offered with mock sincerity. "Well, I'll just be going then. Thank you ever so much for all of your hospitality. You were really the perfect hosts and that homemade blueberry pie was simply the cat's pajamas."

Suffice it to say that I was short-stopped on the way to the parking lot by two of the largest hosts that I have ever seen in a Shop Rite. So, while I could not enjoy any more complimentary items, I did leave the store with quite a few snapshots, and all of my body parts intact. They also made no mention of the fact that I was banned from the store.

Opening the front door to the car, I thanked my burly escorts and felt somewhat satisfied by the results of my mission. I fantasized about the contented feeling that I would get when I would no longer see a *Guest Services* sign at a supermarket. Turning out of the parking lot, two thoughts hit me and abruptly interrupted the warm glow of my future victory.

What exactly is meant by *managed care*? And what the heck are the *cat's pajamas?*

SWETT Equity

September 2007

Dear Readers,

For minutes on end, I've been racking my brain to come up with a column that would entertain you, inform you, and somehow make your day—and that of your cyberneighbor's—just a little brighter. But enough about you. After further review, I have decided to simply mollify some of the inner voices careening through my head and see where they take me this time. It's not easy when your only muses are from within and they speak to you with scratchy voices saying things like, "Try this, asshole."

Love,
Your Self-Centered Friend, Matt

So I would like to share with you an idea I have for a screenplay—or is it a sitcom? Let's just call it a *treatment*. Over the years, I've written a small book or two and a lot of poems and little plays and some other shtick, but I think this will be the first treatment that I haven't received or administered. I'm a little nervous about preparing such a treatment, as I've heard that treatments are subjected to such abusive treatment in Hollywood. My secondary idea is to start a relief organization tentatively called the Society of Writers for the Ethical Treatment of Treatments, or SWETT. I'm getting excited about the possibilities of this column that may lead to the first treatment under the aegis of SWETT. Are you still there, dear readers?

They say to write about what you know, or what you are, so any resemblance to this self-centered author is almost purely intentional. The main character will be a guy who is having a really hard time accepting that he is in his 40s, even though he arrived there more than five years ago. He would love to spend his days still playing ball with the neighborhood *kids*, and then relaxing by watching more sports along with a lot of movies, music, and TV.

He is married to a beautiful woman to whom he is 100 percent faithful except when he is not. Just kidding ... except when he is daydreaming of any number of women whom he has met or almost met over the last thirty years or so. As in *Everybody Loves Raymond*, his family (not sure which characters to unleash here) is highly dysfunctional, but in a more Jewish, Neil Simon-Woody Allen-Jerry Seinfeld, not quite Mel Brooks, sort of way. A la *Raymond*, kids are optional, and only show up once in a while when convenient for a theme or a shtick.

But the focus of this treatment is the protagonist—I'm thinking that his first name should be both common and monosyllabic—and the interactions he has with his colleagues, friends, family members, and inner voices. He works in sales for a large corporation, but it is kind of his own business. He's attracted to the flexibility of his schedule, but he's just not bringing home much bacon, which is okay, because he keeps kosher. No, scratch that thought. It's not really okay, because he resents the mounting bills and pressures and the fact that he has not achieved more in life.

He also resents his wife's resentments, but most of this is handled in a subtle, serious sort of way. There is a lot of levity on the surface, but underlying it are the heavier themes of aging, lost opportunities, and holding onto one's optimism, dignity, and creativity. So, the mood is often light, but there are often retreats into the heavier, if not the darker, side. Or perhaps the prevailing mood can be heavy with occasional humor and levity. I'll do either to advance this project artistically or financially.

Now, while Mr. Monosyllable (John? Dave? Ron?) goes about the daily business of trying to make a living, his caustic, irreverent humor skewers both his colleagues and business account contacts that he also resents. They are unenlightened, boring, and downright selfish—and a majority of them are richer and younger than he is. He often mocks them, but only one other colleague and his wife hear his rants. To his colleagues' knowledge, he is the soul of grace, kindness, generosity, and good humor. So, John/Dave/Ron releases steam by coming up with comedy routines, "top ten" lists, and impersonations that put these antagonists in their place, and his world is somehow restored to its rightful order.

Is this a drama or comedy, you say? Not sure, but I think it's a hybrid. Call it a dramedy, or a *comma*. I'm thinking that if it becomes a sitcom, there would be no live audience or laugh track. Or how about this idea? It's a movie filmed before a live audience, and if they don't laugh at the funny parts, we'll cue in a laugh track.

Back to the premise. What about J/D/R's home life? I'm not sure about the kids and how they might detract from or advance the story. (Thanks for indulging my rough draft, readers.) The wife definitely works, and works hard, and like so many of us, is not in love with what she is doing. Perhaps, she drives a long distance to her job—the eight-plus hours spent mostly in a cubicle, staring at a monitor all day. Her work is technical, but not challenging, and she is capable of so much more creatively and intellectually. She threatens to quit on a weekly basis, trying to light a fire under her husband, yet she doesn't know if that fire would truly move him off his butt or act to consume their savings—and accelerate the ruin of their home and their future.

J/D/R also spends most of his days staring at his monitor, avoiding the prospecting and other sometimes loathsome activities that may lead to more sales, more income, and a cushier home and bank account. No matter where he has worked before or currently—social service agencies, schools, or other sales positions—he has often tried hard, yet he has never had a position that he truly devoted his heart and soul to. Something has always gotten in his way—be it incompetent supervisors, stifling atmospheres, ignorant, downright objectionable colleagues, and/or low pay.

At his monitor, he sends the occasional e-mail to a colleague or would-be account and does his paperwork, but the other 80 percent of the time he is spending on sports and movie sites or on YouTube. Oh yeah, he does some writing on the side.

His mind often takes him—Walter Mitty-like—into new worlds that challenge him, excite him, and bring him much more acclaim and fortune than the real world. But even in his dreams, he is too much the pessimist to ever taste what he is starving for.

In one of these dream sequences, he is the head writer for an advertising agency. You see, even his dreams are pretty dull. He is working for Nike or a Nike-like shoe/sportswear giant that is searching for the perfect, pithy slogan that captures the feeling of empowerment they wish to project. After hours of brainstorming, he comes up with the idea that speaks to a whole new market—"Just ruminate on the possibility of thinking about doing something different today." He thinks it is perfect and explains to his boss and the Nike people that it would open their products to a whole new demographic—the intellectual and introspective would–be weekend warriors who have been intimidated prior to now. Of course, the sequence ends with his demotion to the department store print ad department, where his cube is parked under a giant *Just Do It* banner.

But after years and years of unfulfilled dreams, our hero—is the name "Matt" okay?— strikes it rich when his lines of eco-friendly bumper stickers, greeting cards, and fortune cookies take the world by storm. The scores of millions he has earned allow him to move with his wife and optional family to a home so immense that it has a name but no address. They immediately celebrate by brainstorming a bunch of new names for their mansion while bikini-clad handywomen are changing all the toilet seats.

Fulfilling a promise made to his wife (note to self: do I use her real name?), he has used his fortune to also buy homes in the neighborhood for the rest of his wife's family—a move that he will regret for the length of this movie/TV series. He occasionally will pay the freight for his own family to fly in for visits— Jewish holidays, April Fools' Days, and Super Bowls—and he will certainly have second thoughts each time he does so.

With all the money he will ever need for five lifetimes, he spends his days playing softball, tennis, basketball, and ping-pong with his buddies, when not complaining about his injuries, clipping coupons, watching YouTube or contemplating writing some treatments. He and his wife soon achieve the type of intimacy they have always dreamed about and even watch movies together in the same home theatre two or three times a week.

So, my fellow readers and writers, my inner voices have suddenly gone silent, and that's all I've got so far. I think I'll share this premise at my inaugural SWETT meeting. Until we meet again, may all your treatments be treated with kindness.

If a Book Falls in Collingswood ... ?

October/November 2007

A bright blue pastel flier arrived in the mail today, requesting my attendance at the fourth annual Collingswood (New Jersey) Book Festival, an event for no-name authors, never heard-of publishers, and all around swell people. Never heard of it? Don't worry; you're in good company. Before filling out the tear sheet with my reply, I thought back to my experience last October.

As last year was my third as a writer/vendor, I was well prepared for the crush of cultured Collingswoodians that figured to flood the Main Street-like Collings Avenue to support us local scribes. In the past, my wife Ruby and I had arrived all bundled up in the early morning, gradually peeling off layers of casual clothes to be in harmony with the brilliant early fall afternoons. Great weather, the opportunity to discuss my couple books with the throngs of literati that visited us, and a better-than-average Collings Avenue pizzeria all awaited us.

We were excited for our third festival and had lined up everything we could think of the day before prior to heading to New York City to visit her family. We actually had even made our bed and set up three alarm clocks for the early morning wakeup call. I am past the age where I can comfortably pull an all-nighter and 6:45 am was a wakeup time that had earned my grudging admiration and contempt.

After stuffing ourselves on her family's delicious homemade Chinese food, we returned to our Cherry Hill home at 2:00 am. Less than five hours of sleep remained when Ruby had an idea that would no doubt stimulate book sales. She had a collection of thirty beautiful, decorative bookmarks that her sister had previously sent her from China. It was her inspired marketing plan that any Collingswoodian who bought two or more of my books would receive a free bookmark, for which she made a little display by poking metal hooks into a spongy base covered with some candy corn of unknown vintage. My anticipatory lack of sleep was now overpowered by a sense of greed.

Dressed as Underwear Man, I typed out a sign that proclaimed that my adoring public could buy any two books—already discounted by the way—and receive a free, beautiful bookmark. I added, quite cagily, three other words to the sign—*while supplies last.* I was already doing the math: *2 books for $18 times 30 = $540.* The sixty books we would sell—conservatively speaking of course—would eclipse our 2004 personal record by about forty-eight books or so. There was the $25 registration fee we had to pay, and the gas, coffee, and junk food bills. But nevertheless it figured to be a profitable day in the old town.

Tired and clad in my unmentionables, I decided that it was too dark, cold, and wet to pack the car now. No, I would go to bed dry and almost rich. I kissed my generous, fellow marketing genius good night and was asleep within two minutes. Possibly another personal record.

About five seconds later, the cacophony of three cheap alarm clocks interrupted my slumber. *How could I forget to stagger the alarm times*? I admonished myself as I staggered out of bed. I quickly washed and shaved without waking up Ruby—the definition of a mean feat, as it is reliably reported that she could sleep through an air raid siren if she needed to. Since it was cold, dark, and wet, and since I had no choice, I started jamming my *writerly* belongings into the car. Yes, I had everything—the six-foot table, which made it into the car on my thirteenth attempt, my display board, writing tablets, pens, and business cards. What else? I found a little space for the most important stuff—my books and the invaluable and beautiful decorative bookmarks. Everything was stuffed in with as much love and affection as I could muster under the circumstances.

The car jam-packed, I roused the marketing guru out of bed, who greeted her lack of restorative sleep in tolerably good humor. Within ten minutes, and brandishing a small thermos of coffee, Ruby found just enough room under the long table to squeeze into the passenger seat. Ten minutes later, with windshield wipers and headlights fully activated, we arrived on a semi-deserted and fully dampened Collings Avenue.

A fortyish man, protected by a bright orange poncho, saw our overloaded compact car and waved for us to stop. He then directed us to Collingswood High School, the rain venue for the event. I greeted the news with ambivalence, as a man of my conflicted nature is wont to do—well, most of the time. On the bright side, I wouldn't have to worry about gusts of winds knocking over my display board, as they constantly did last year. On the dark side, what about the throngs of readers who welcomed a nice early autumn day, live music, and open shops nearby? Would they pack Collingswood High, and once there, be in the mood to buy some cleverly worded books of poetry and humor?

To say the least, I was anxious to see which side would win out.

While Ruby sat in a double-parked car, ignoring the taunts of traffic cops and other writer/entrepreneurs, I started to unload my car, placing my inventory and marketing tools just outside the entrance to the school's *cafetorium*. (Presumably, there is not an *audeteria* at the high school.) One of the festival volunteers—identifiable by her advanced age, officious nature, and fake smile—told me that I should look for my booth number (eighty-two), which was located outside the cafetorium, around another hallway, and then down a short flight of stairs. Number eighty-two, logically enough, was situated right across from number forty-seven, and in a little fifteen-by-fifteen foot area in between another flight of stairs that led to the gymnasium (Go, Panthers!), more classrooms, and some well-placed lavatories.

After showing Ruby where we would be stationed, I parked my car across the street while she guarded our little store. Despite the rainy weather and half my brain envisioning a long day in Pantherland, I was excited to unpack and set up shop. Ruby left to go to Philly for an appointment; her navigation as uncanny as ever, she would make it back shortly before the close of the festival.

There was still one hour before the festival would open its doors to the public. Needing the brisk exercise, I sprung into action, attempting to give my space just the right amount of feng shui to pry smiles and dollars from the enchanted passersby. I found that it was a pleasure to set up my three-panel display board at just the right angle without worrying about the destructive gale forces that kept toppling it in years past. My brochures would also not get damp or lost, and I could arrange my poetry and humor books just so.

No doubt, the Chinese bookmarks would lend just the right amount of beauty and the *while supplies last* sign would add the perfect sense of urgency. Yes, there seemed to be a perfect collision of art and commerce that morning in the little town of Collingswood, proud gateway to the borough of Haddon Heights.

Evidently, the lighter side of my mood was winning out, a rare event for a self-indulgent poet. Soon, I was even rationalizing that it would not be such a bad thing that the new location would be out of walking distance from the pizza shop that caught my fancy last year. That meant that there would be fewer distractions for the festival visitors who would be my literary captives. And I sure did not need all the empty calories that the pizza parlor would provide. Besides, booth number ninety-five had free candy bars and there was even a hot dog cart parked right outside.

It's always nice to hedge your bets if the going gets rough. And even if I did pig out on dogs, fries, cookies, and candy bars, I noticed that it was about 115 degrees within a 20-foot radius of my spot—the calories would burn off instantly. I was starting to get dizzy from all this circular reasoning, so I decided that I would take a walk. Fifteen minutes or so still remained before show time and it was nice to be able to visit a high school lav without needing a hall pass.

On the way to the lav, I popped by number ninety-five, feigned interest in the civic program they were promoting, and asked meekly if I could grab a Hershey's bar or three. First mission accomplished. I then peeked inside the gym, where tables and tent cards were set up for local celebrities to sign their books. While chewing on a Hershey's Almond, I envisioned myself in the corner of the gym underneath a banner celebrating a 1962 Panthers conference basketball championship. Microphone in hand, I was giving a reading to a group of enthralled local readers dressed in their most fashionable raincoats.

"Matt Goldberg, author of several books, including the best-selling *So So Wisdom*, has braved the elements to be with us today. This award-hoarding, nationally syndicated humor columnist has graciously deigned to give us a short reading." Well, I could wait on the exact wording of the introduction, but I could not wait to get to the lav.

For a forty-four-year-old bathroom, the facilities were not too bad. I wondered what shenanigans went on nowadays in these facilities. While my dark side longed for the good old days where the *cooler* kids (of which I was not a member) would sneak in a smoke or two of varying lengths, my light side hoped that this era of Panthers was a little smarter. It was time to dry my hands and alas there was no rotating towel or any paper products in sight. Yes, it was time to choose between ripping off a square of toilet paper or trying my luck with the electric hand dryer—a luxury item that Lenape High School (Go, Native Americans!) did not offer back in the day.

Choosing the technological route, I prepared to arrange my hands in just the right angle to coax a waft of breeze from the device. Usually, I fare rather poorly with even the crudest bathroom innovations. On many a turnpike restroom visit, I have watched as strangers cruise through the hand-drying lane like cocky E-Z Pass users. When it is my turn, I try everything from NFL referee motions to elaborate semaphore signals to no avail. As the strangers behind me vent their displeasure, I invariably slap my dampened hands on my jeans on the way to the vending machines.

Fifteen feet from the dryer, I did some stretching exercises to prepare myself for the task ahead. Feeling limber and confident, I decided to go with the simple, palm-up method that rarely had worked for me before. As my trusted memory is my only witness, the most amazing indoor meteorological event in South Jersey history was about to take place. At the eight-foot mark, the little white unit sensed my wet hands and let loose a blast of warm air that nearly pushed me into stall number two. Regaining my balance, my dry hands and I walked out of the lav and prepared to clasp palms with my generous and grateful readership. Little did I know then that my experience with Hurricane Latrina would be the highlight of my day.

With an extra hop in my step, I returned to table eighty-two, checking out my literary exhibit from all possible angles. The display board showcased a nice caricature of *So So Gai*—my fictitious, irreverent Chinese philosopher—along with samples of his mediocre philosophy and a chronology of his life and times. Flanking the board on the table were piles of books and brochures advertising my services as a speaker, copies of one of my poems, and samples of So So Gai's wisdom. My new business cards were sprinkled around the bookmarks and the clever sign on the far side of the table, so the Collingswoodians would see it before ascending the stairs to the gymnasium and the bathrooms. I greeted the 10:00 am opening with positive anticipation as I noticed that there was still no occupant across the way in number forty-seven.

What follows are my hourly recollections of the fourth annual Collingswood Book Festival:

Hour #1: During the first forty-five minutes or so, I had plenty of time to sweat in the *sauna-torium* where I was stationed. The crowd had not started to arrive in earnest, so I also had plenty of time to rearrange my book display and crack my knuckles. A few people stopped by and laughed at a couple of So So Gai-isms, but they did not feel the urge to buy his wisdom—even at the discounted rate with personalized messages from the author. A couple kids asked if it was okay to eat some of the candy corn. I mentioned, in vain, that it was for display purposes only and I could not vouch for its cleanliness. By the end of the hour, the green sponge that was the base for the bookmark hangers was starting to reveal itself. Ruby phoned near the end of the hour to inform me that she was on the way back to Collingswood. Book sales were stagnant.

Hour #2: I had plenty of time to look up at the ceiling and noticed a few tiles missing, revealing a slew of exposed electrical wires. Hey, if I wanted to see that, I could have stayed home and tried to sell books from my garage. The pace of readers was starting to pick up. Most would glance at my display on the way up the stairs to the gymnasium or on the way downstairs to the children's area in the high school basement. I started to engage in more conversations with the locals that would linger a little while at my store. Some grabbed business cards and brochures; another guy remembered me from last year and honored his proud tradition of laughing at my book but refusing to buy any copies. Still others noticed my Eagles cap and talked a little football with me. Never a bad thing.

Near the end of the hour, a young cutie with a tiny fistful of candy corn in her mouth asked me if she could have one of the bookmarks. The ogre in me politely explained that I could not give one to her but that they were free with the purchase of any two of my books. After conferring with her parents, she asked if she could buy one for a dollar. In a less polite fashion, I declined her generous offer. Taking inventory after two hours, I observed that while book sales were flat, there was a decent run on free brochures and business cards. But help was on its way. Ruby called to ask me if she could bring me a toasted sesame bagel.

"Of course," I said, basking in the near presence of my wife and a snack that had always been good to me.

Hour #3: I was nothing if not prepared, supply-wise, for the event. The day before, I had started reading John Grogan's *Marley and Me*, and I brought it along in case business wasn't brisk. For the rest of the day, the cover shot of Marley was placed between my own books and the display board. Hey, even if I could not mislead the yokels into finding a connection between my book and this lovable bestseller, I could at least enjoy a quick discussion about the joys and rigors of dog ownership. As a marketing ploy, it worked like a hex.

As the day moved on toward halftime, I found it more difficult to suppress my dark side. Sure, I helped parents carry their strollers up the stairs and I directed a lot of people to the gym, but a certain acrimony had taken hold of me. To those who I thought could handle the humor, I started yelling like a Philly carnival barker.

"Yo, step on up, and find a bunch of overpriced books that really suck." Some enjoyed the humor, but those same people apparently did not have any disposable income with them.

In between phone calls to Ruby, I started writing out a new sign that would change my fortune. Something drastic and ingenious was needed: my inventory of books and bookmarks had not changed, and even the free candy corn was only depleted by half.

Hour #4: My new sign was a masterstroke of genius, if I do say so myself. It read, in bold, black Sharpie lettering, as follows:

With the Purchase of a Beautiful Bookmark from China

Discounted to $18

You May Choose Any Two Books For Free!

Much as the sign seemed to bolster my flagging spirits, in due time I wondered if I had just hit the final frontier of indignity. Yes, a few people seemed to be amused by the sign, but they rewarded me with laughter—not greenbacks.

After only a half hour, I put the sign away for a less rainy day. My main conversations with the public involved telling some high school–aged kids that, yes, they could eat the candy corn with my compliments. In a jaded moment, I may have even mentioned that it was homemade and good for their teeth.

A breakthrough did come shortly after I retired the sign. A fiftyish woman of obvious good taste leafed through my book of poetry and actually started pulling money from her purse. A sight of an actual dead president coming my way made me a little weak in the knees, but somehow I remained upright. I accepted it graciously, signed my book, and was about to french kiss the lady, when I spotted my beautiful bride carrying a bagel bag.

Hour # 5: Ruby handed me the bag, which I ripped open to reveal a cold, untoasted plain bagel topped with a smattering of butter. I accepted it in the best spirit and probably mumbled something unintelligible when she asked me how things were going. I figured that she could do the math.

Realizing that we were overstaffed, my better half asked me if she could get me something else to eat. Not mentioning my trips to booth number ninety-five and the hot dog cart, I said that I could use a hot dog and a hot chocolate. (I am happy to report that Ruby did not get lost to or from the hot dog vendor.)

With more time on my hands, I searched for instant perspective on what was going wrong with my marketing aspirations. Why had my delusions of grandeur been downgraded to dreams of solvency?

I decided—sour grapes or not—that there were only three groups of people that tended to actually sell a fair amount of books at these events:

1. The "I've heard of that guy/lady" author, who had achieved some name recognition in at least some of the local Philadelphia-area households. The ones with the tables, tent cards, and microphone access.
2. The people who were selling grab bags of gently mangled books for $.50 or $1, so the bargain hunters could fill up their plastic bags with these clearance items.
3. The authors who told all their friends. I also told all my friends but am ashamed to tell you that neither of them had the courtesy to show up.

In between bites and sips of hot dog and warm chocolate, I did manage to sell a humor book or two and had another very sincere lady ask me how long I would be there, as she would go to the Mac machine in the meantime. A wise veteran of such conversations, I knew that I would never see Ms. Sincerity again.

Hour #6: The homestretch had arrived, and neither the few recent book sales nor my instant perspective were doing much to ward off my dark side. I vowed to stay until the end of the event, even as other booksellers were starting to fold their tables. After all, I am a Philly sports fan at heart who never leaves a game early despite the margin of victory or deficit. Ruby started packing up some of my stuff as my lack of sleep and surplus of bad mood was taking my mind elsewhere.

In my daydream, I found myself in the midst of the new musical *Collingswood*—a newly minted parody of *Chicago*. In this town of big spenders who don't read, and big readers who don't spend, I had become an incarnation of the invisible Amos. Here I was, the one-and-only *Mr. Sell-Nothing*! The refrain was running through my head as the Collingswoodians refrained from buying my books. I did all I could to stop from singing my new showstopper out loud:

Sell-nothing / I'm Mr. Sell-Nothing
Won't you buy something / So I can wear some bling
But you just walk right past me/ and look right through me
And never buy a thing...

(I was really starting to roll now)

So, Mr. Hicktown shnook / Won't you buy my book
Are you afraid to look ...

When Ruby interrupted my hit musical with a request that we leave ten minutes early—like almost everyone else—I found no rationale to protest. We packed up all our stuff and I started the end-of-the-day trudge through the cafetorium. I made several trips outside the high school with my precious few belongings, putting blind faith in the belief that although the locals did not buy any books, they were also not the type to steal any.

Pleased with this bit of logic, I made my last trip to booth number eighty-two, when I looked up to see Ms. Sincerity and a friend waiting for me. "Matt, I was afraid you would leave, and I wouldn't get a copy of your book," this paragon of virtue said with a smile.

"Oh, I wouldn't leave without seeing you first," I said with all the false conviction I could manage. I looked around to see one carton of unopened humor books, from which I happily pried one loose. For one of the few times that day, I signed my collector's item and wished her a good day. If the bookmarks weren't on the sidewalk, I would have thrown in a few of those as well.

Returning to the sidewalk, Ruby's car arrived almost on cue. Working together like Forrest and Bubba, we somehow were able to jam in the very same items that we had stuffed in early that morning. Taking the wheel of the car, I could barely see my marketing partner, obscured as she was by the table. Mr. Sell-Nothing or not, I tried my best to provide some cheer for my wife, for myself, and for unknown authors everywhere.

"You know," I said, most likely sounding somewhat like a fighter after losing a championship bout, "if you factor out the gas, the

bagels, the hot dogs, and the hot chocolate, and you don't count the money I spent for my own books, I think we made a little money again this year, honey."

Our six-foot table seemed to shake in agreement, behind which my wife had evidently dozed off. Perhaps the love of my life was dreaming what I was thinking: If we get our registration fee in a little earlier next year, we can secure a prime spot in the cafetorium should it rain. As dreams go, it wasn't much, but it did get us home safely from Collingswood.

The Quizzical Nature of Blank Pages

December 2007

As November is about to expire, I am facing a deadline, a mostly blank yellow tablet (save the previous sixteen words) and the imaginary, impatient faces of a readership that I am grateful to have an opportunity to write for. Indeed, I am thankful that Thanksgiving, Black Friday, and all the pickings of a delicious turkey have all passed without incident and I am now somewhat thankful that my nonprolific butt doesn't have to write this column more than once a month. I say this even as I dream about writing columns much more frequently and eventually meeting and conversing with more of you—the aforementioned imaginary, impatient faces.

With my deadline imminent, if not yet ignored, my internal muse tells me that I should not only write on, but also about, blank pages. This may be because in the past month or so, I've typed thousands of quasi-creative e-mails and written the occasional delightful greeting card, but this is the first time that I've tried to draft a complete column with just pen and paper.

It wasn't so long ago that using pen and paper was the only way to write creatively. (By paper, I mean any object that leaves room for my penned thoughts, my "fave five" consisting of spiral notebooks, legal pads, envelopes, white spaces on print ads, and ATM receipts.) I'm not exactly sure why, but my supposition is that it has something to do with the organic nature of the writing process. My thoughts and words just felt much more genuine when I was putting pen or crayon to legal pad or rumpled envelope.

It used to be the case that there was even more of a disconnect between my left/right brain and the two fingers I was typing with. Every time I had to return the carriage on my Olympia typewriter, I lost my train of thought. More recently, since I graduated to four-finger typing with computer screens, the problem was that it was harder to claim ownership of words that appeared on a screen, as opposed to those jotted feverishly on a parking ticket. Now it seems that I prefer the four-finger typing method. Is it because there is less of a disconnect now between my thoughts and my typed words? Or is it because both my penmanship and eyesight have worsened? I hope that the answer is not that I prefer not to claim ownership of my words now. I say this as I have decided to abandon my semilegible legal pad for the convenience and objectivity of my desktop.

Having now typed all this, I wish to elicit the expertise of our writing community with some of the questions that my blank pages and screens have inspired. I will do this in the form of a short quiz, without an answer key or a "what-this-all-means" decoder. Along the way, I will probably throw in the occasional anecdote that may illuminate my own approaches. By the way, I just completed an "Are you a right-brained or left-brained" quiz online, only to find out that I'm 29 percent right, 20 percent left, and 51 percent scatterbrained.

In this reader participation exercise, I will precede each question with the word "Quiz" written in bold and followed by a colon—an homage of sorts to how my brothers and I would interact and still do on occasion. We might all be sitting there watching TV or eating dinner, when one of us would blurt out "Quiz," capturing the others' full attention. The question could then range from the patently obvious (Quiz: In what year did Columbus discover America?) to the arcane factoid (Quiz: Who was Zachary Taylor's vice president?) to the totally trivial, yet kind of factual (**Quiz:** What type of car is Mr. Sharkey thinking about buying?), to the self-indulgently subjective (**Quiz**: What are my three favorite sitcoms of all time?).

So let's begin with these guidelines. When I write "I", I mean "you"; you don't have to tell me your answers, but you're invited to give feedback. You don't have to show me your work. Okay ...

Quiz: I am feeling most creative when I am:
a) writing with good old-fashioned pen and paper
b) typing on my desktop
c) typing on my laptop
d) writing or typing my tax returns
e) it depends on the type of writing

My answer would be anything but "c," as the only laptop I use for these purposes is a legal pad on top of my jeans while sitting on the couch. My best answer currently may be "e," as I still prefer to write poetry with pen and paper, even though I've graduated to "b" otherwise.

Quiz: When staring at a blank page/screen, I:
a) am excited about all the possibilities
b) am feeling great pressure to produce
c) am ecstatic for a nanosecond, until I convince myself that I'll screw it up

d) have the emotionless expectation that I'll probably leave it blank before escaping to my TV, e-mail, or favorite Web site

For those who went with "a," do you feel the same way before moving into an unfurnished apartment or house? I am definitely a "c" in those situations. While I have a little more confidence in my writing than my decorating, I vacillate terribly between all the choices.

Let me share an anecdote that will betray my age, my approach to college, and my somewhat devious and logical mind. It has to do with blank pages and I don't know if I'm confessing or bragging. Once upon a time in college at a supposedly prestigious *anonymous* Ivy League school in Philly, my Poly Sci professor assigned a take-home exam that had to be turned in at a specific time and place. Procrastinating to the very end, I remember driving across the bridge to my parents' house and hurriedly giving myself about two hours to write out my answers before having to drive back to Philly. Realizing that I would not have time to complete the exam (less a case of writers block than my being a jackass), my paper magically skipped from the bottom of page four to the top of page seven—which started in the middle of a sentence that set up my concluding paragraph.

If I remember correctly, I turned it in unstapled, and may have even put shoeprints on the bottom of a few of the pages. My memory says that I either got a "B" or a "mulligan" on the exam. Ah, the power of the blank page(s). The missing page caper suggests my next question.

Quiz: In my life, I have only cheated on/at:
a) school assignments and tests

b) golf, but doesn't everybody?
c) the aforementioned tax returns
d) all of the above, and ... never mind
e) how dare you assail my integrity!

As this isn't *Dr. Phil*, allow me to move on to one final topic that may or may not help me/us to fill in more blank pages in the future.

Quiz: Writing-wise, I am most productive when:
a) I write at specific, scheduled times and utilize an outline
b) I write at a specific time and place, no outline needed
c) I use an outline, at whatever time and place
d) I'm a streak hitter; I'm much better when I wing it and just go with the flow
e) writing at a specific time; place is optional
f) writing from a specific place; the time is optional
g) "Huh?!"

I'm not into interpreting other people's answers, but if you were looking for an "all of the above" option, your writing career/hobby may be temporarily on thin ice. Not to worry, as all of the options seemed perfectly palatable to me, and I choose to regard this as a sign of open-mindedness and creativity.

Before signing off and wishing you a happy December and many beautifully filled pages, let me leave you with two final thoughts:

1) If you answered "g" to all four of the questions, you are either very creative or skipped the first three questions.
2) The answers to my semi-hypothetical family quiz questions are:

- The patently obvious—1492 (come on!)
- The arcane factoid—Millard Fillmore, for about fifteen months
- The totally trivial—back in the day, a Plymouth Fury
- The self-indulgently subjective—as of now, *The Honeymooners, All In The Family,* and *Seinfeld*

Happy December!

2008

Resolutionary Ideas

January 2008

Different Year, Same Old Shirt? That's about the size of it, or has it shrunk over time and relative to my expansion?

New Year, Same Old Shift? But what is my shift, and is it steady or constantly shifting? It's probably a combination of the two. And speaking of shifts, is it better to be shiftless or shifty? If I stopped being shiftless, would my writing be more shifty? Would I be praised for a real *shifty* column? Can I avoid these puns and keep my trains of thought? Maybe in 2009.

For 2008, I say I want a resolution. Make that plural; I need some resolutions. I've only written about five sets of New Year's resolutions over the years and like most of us, I've found that they're pretty easy to make and very easy to break. Yet I feel compelled to make a new and improved list of resolutions for my shifty new column. I may be tired, but I don't want to be listless. With apologies to John Lennon, I say I want a resolution. Well, you know …

My Resolutions for 2008

Feed My Creativity and Be More Productive. Hey, that's vague and intangible enough. How will I measure my 2008 creativity and production at this time next year? Not easily, which means that I'm not bound to flunk this one on my end-of-the-year score sheet. Also, I'm sure that most people don't have this at the top of their list. Points earned for creativity. This one's a keeper.

Be Adventuresome; Try New Things. This isn't quite the same as number one, as I should be open-minded enough to try new things that have nothing to do with my desire to be more productive. Adventure for adventure's sake. Meet new people, help more people through volunteer work. Read new books, see more world cinema, and listen to more world music. (Except for that New Age crap.) I didn't say that, did I? Ignore that one, please. On second thought, I'll have to reconsider this goal as I don't want to change my essential nature. Or do I?

Be More Consistent. This is kind of an old standby, even if it doesn't add points to my creativity score. Having worked many sales jobs with a modicum of success, I have always been told—ad nauseum—that it's all about consistency. With consistent effort (one can only really control one's effort, right?) comes more productivity. Quite frankly, I have consistently failed to be very consistent in my work habits—especially in my writing habits. So that means that I need to change and not be so consistent. No, I need to change in order to be more consistent. This means that I truly need to be more adventuresome and try new things.

But since I'm reconsidering that goal, let me move on to the next one.

Lose Weight. No ... that's too vague, and weight is a tangible item. **Lose fifteen pounds.** Can I find fifteen new pounds first? Sorry. I think I can spare the fifteen, if not seventeen, and I've done it before. But since I tend to only maintain diet and exercise regimens for no more than two months, I really shouldn't start on this goal until November 1. Shouldn't all goals be realistic and timely? Okay, starting November 1, 2008, I will do the things I need to do to lose fifteen pounds by year's end. As I currently am about a paper clip shy of 200 pounds, it will be nice to visit the 180s again.

The only possible problem here is that I really do wish to keep all of my other goals—even the ones that I had been reconsidering. What good is a list of resolutions without at least seven items on the list? And if I'm going to keep my goal of meeting new people—my wife and I have discussed and agreed on this—wouldn't it be ungracious of us to not invite them over to our house? I can't invite them over and not have food for them. A lot of food. Or maybe we'll try some new restaurants and enjoy some world cinema over some American popcorn. Alternately, we can just hang out and discuss some great new books while listening to some new music. *Veg* out on some meat, potato chips, and chocolate. I guess we can do it in a more heart-healthy way, but do I really want to hang out with a bunch of undernourished people who listen to that New Age crap?

Something's gotta give here, but I'll leave this one on my list. I have till November to work out the details.

Take More Interest in Current Events and Issues That Don't Directly Affect Me but Probably Really

Do if I Look at Things in a More Unselfish, Long-Term, Global Sort Of Way. I believe in writing goals that are very easy to remember and I also believe that bumper stickers are way too small. That being said, I have embarrassed myself in the past year or so by not being more conversant with issues that really matter. You know, like Amy Winehouse's latest stint in rehab. No, no, no, I don't mean the pop culture tabloid fodder—which both sickens me, and um, nauseates me in an addictive kind of way—but the real stories and issues that should matter to all of us. World peace, poverty, joblessness, homelessness, and global warming are all issues that I really care about but find myself too lazy and jaded to even do my little bit toward solving. And half the time, I don't even bother to read or listen to any in-depth discussions of domestic and world events.

So my goal here is to be better informed and find out how I can contribute more to the world. I guess I have time to work out the details here as well. At minimum, here's something that's been on my mind. With all of the coverage of the Iowa Caucus, New Hampshire Primary, and all things Presidential Election 2008, I've been drawn to the political horse race—just as I have been every four years. I'm not sure which horse I'll be backing, but if past voting loyalties hold, I'm 99.99 percent sure that I'll choose a *donkey* over an *elephant*. Now, which jackass will I choose?

As I've gotten lazier, I tend to fall prey to a certain kind of thinking that the media seems to encourage. When a significant world event occurs—such as the assassination of Benazir Bhutto—the emphasis seems to be on what effect this incident will have on the chances of the various candidates. Instead, shouldn't the focus be more on what each of the candidates would do in a given situation? Taking my cue from the media and my own inertia, I tend to follow the horse race instead of projecting what each of the horses will do based on their track records and the platforms that have come from those horses' mouths (or nether regions). So let's put this on my slightly outsized 2008 bumper sticker:

Be Enlightened, Stay Enlightened, and Say "Nay" to Bad, Incompetent, or Evil Horses.
With six items on my list of resolutions, even though the wording of most of the items hasn't been resolved, let me add a final one that is not original. I don't remember who to attribute it to. Yes, "do more detailed research" was not one of my 2007 goals. So with thanks to someone whose words, if not his name, made an impression on me, here it is:

Value Happiness Instead of Self-Righteousness.
Talk about a tough one for me. It's so easy to get self-righteous over so many things, both in the world and in my personal universe. If I felt powerful enough to change all the things out there that make me feel either disrespected, ignored, frustrated, or depressed, then I wouldn't be prone to feeling so self-righteous. And, I'd also be a lot happier. On second thought, I'd probably lose a lot of ideas for columns and poems and screenplays if I became too content. Can I really write shiny, happy poems and columns when my unofficial motto has been "Suffering is mandatory; pain is optional"?

Besides, I say to my imaginary antagonists, it's kind of fun to be self-righteous. Why shouldn't I be? What, you think you're so much better?

Well, now that I've kind of sketched out seven realistic goals for 2008—okay, about five of them need some work—I wish you and all those important to you a very Happy New Year. And, I'll try to do the same in my own creative, adventuresome, consistent, skinny, current, enlightened, happy, and self-righteous way.

That's all for now, friends. Time to work on those *egantic* new bumper stickers.

Agents for Change

February 2008

We're only a couple of months into our newest reality show titled *Presidential Campaign 2008: The Amazing Race for the White House*, but the show has been must-see TV since the very start. Its ratings will never approach *American Idol* numbers, but that's okay given the older demographic that such a show attracts. In fact, you may remember that this show piloted in 2004 with the title *White House 2004: Anybody but Bush*, which was won, ironically, by a guy named George W Bush.

Apparently, they tried to pilot a similar series in 2000, but it wasn't picked up until after the votes were already counted. Well, most of the votes were counted, except for the ones in Florida, where all of the networks joined forces to coproduce a six-week show called *Hanging Chad Meets Katherine Harris*. It made for pretty good drama, featuring interesting places like Broward County and less interesting people—including a man named Jeb.

Hanging Chad even showed us an overweight Al Gore playing touch football with his children on his front lawn for the first time ever. As a result of global warming, or maybe his 113 extra pounds, Gore was jogging around in the middle of November wearing nothing more than a T-shirt. The levity was appreciated but each day as the votes were being counted to determine the winner, millions of viewers and thousands of chads were left hanging. Poor Al was runner-up to Bush that year, but I remember him finally giving a concession speech promising to stop playing football. He also pledged to keep nudging us to also conserve our energy until he won the Nobel Prize. Sure, like that was going to happen!

Back to 2008. As I'm writing, candidates such as Joe Biden and Chris Dodd were written off before the 2008 series even aired, and now they've officially been voted off. We've seen primaries and something called a caucus—with differing procedures for the Democratic jackasses and the Republican elephants—who supposedly won't oppose one another until they prevail over fellow members of their species. There has even been a contest in a place called Wyoming—I think it's one of our fifty states—but it wasn't covered in prime time so I don't know if it even existed. Kind of like the proverbial tree in the forest, or for my most loyal readers, a book that falls in Collingswood, New Jersey.

Most of the candidates go from state to state pandering to the locals while speaking in as many generalities as possible. I've found that none of them care too much for Bush; none of the elephants even mention his name and the jackasses imply that he's both as stubborn as an ox, and as dumb as, well, a jackass. After that, it starts getting just a little confusing for this avid viewer. All of the candidates, Republicans and Democrats alike, seem to be saying the same thing while straining themselves to find different ways to say it. The universal message: "I am the candidate for change." With everyone from Clinton to Obama to Huckabee to Romney, and McCain (not to mention

Giuliani, Edwards, Thompson, and Paul) promising change, how do I select the best agent for change? And if I lock in on just one candidate without changing my own mind, am I embracing a lack of change? How do I extricate myself from this philosophical quagmire? It doesn't take much to drive me nuts and this paradox does the trick.

Assuming I make peace with this philosophical dilemma, I have to somehow choose the person who, once he assumes the unofficial designation of leader of the free world, will truly change things for the better. A difficult task, but now that I've been watching several episodes of *Presidential Campaign 2008*, I think I know the best way to do so. I will pick someone with as little inside experience as humanly possible.

Americans seem to like the idea of picking someone who has not been inside the Washington Beltway. So one lesson I've learned is that if vying to be the most powerful person in the free world (I love writing "free world" by the way), you should accentuate your lack of experience within that setting. There seem to be a lot of mayors and former governors running again, some hailing from states situated more than one thousand miles from Washington, DC. Maybe in future seasons we will expand our search to include contestants from foreign countries or distant galaxies. I'm sure they'd make vastly superior agents for change.

And what about the unlucky souls who have been stuck inside the Beltway laboring as congressmen or senators? It's been a long time since one of them has won the presidential dream job, but it appears that the most successful tactic for any of these insiders is either to: a) lie or exaggerate about what they have accomplished, or b) be proud of doing little or nothing, and claim no responsibility for the little they have done—a decent strategy when the states of our economy, education, environment, and foreign policy are all screwed up.

Being a contestant for residency in the White House is very tricky business, even for those who have never held office inside the Beltway. Take 1996 as an example. When Bill Clinton ran for president, he had a head start—being a governor and saxophone player from Arkansas. Yet he faced a totally new challenge. He was roundly criticized by several other candidates for always wanting to be president of the United States. Imagine that! This criticism took me by surprise and seemed to jolt my system to the core. Being an inside-the-box thinker then, I did not even consider the fact that a doctor, plumber, forest ranger, or even a town councilman with no further ambition would make a much better candidate for president. So as of 1996, vision and ambition now joined experience, competence, and accountability as qualities detrimental to being a serious contestant for the presidency. Of course, I was relieved to find out that an ego the size of Alaska was, and is, still considered a good thing.

Another problem to solve: This intrepid, but confusing, new definition of "qualified" was squarely at odds with one of the little jokes I remembered from *The Encyclopedia of Jewish Humor*—a book that my family and I used to read aloud from. I don't know where this book is now, but I'll give you the gist of the joke:

Herbie Mandelbaum, past his prime and dressed shabbily, schleps into a large corporation and approaches the receptionist, demanding to see the personnel director. No one else is worthy of his time.

When the director presents himself, Herbie asks him, "Did you advertise in the New York Times for an MBA with a doctorate in analytical mathematics and extensive experience in statistical analysis and multinational finance?"

"Yes, we did," replies the startled personnel director.

"Well, then," says Mandelbaum, "I want you should know, on me you can't count."

The problem with telling this joke today is that people would wonder why Mandelbaum would give up so easily. With our presidential elections as our guideposts, why should Mandelbaum count himself out just because he lacks a little experience? If I were his job coach, I would tell him the following:

- Keep your chutzpah and your self-deprecating sense of humor; just dress slightly better
- Play up your lack of experience and don't worry yourself or others about what you did or didn't achieve
- Promise change; chances are the corporation or organization is as screwed up as this country is
- Adopt a much more sizeable ego, yet don't burden yourself and others with too much true vision or ambition

My final tip of "The Tip of the Goldberg": To get the position we want—whether on a reality show or in real life (the lines are so blurred now, who can even tell the difference?)—we all should learn from the Huckabees, Clintons, McCains, and Obamas of the world, while still embracing our inner Mandelbaums.

... For Best Waste of Time by a Grown Man, the Oscar Goes To ...

March 2008

If my memory serves its most important purpose—that of, in the parlance of Roger Clemens, not *misremembering*—I should both thank and curse my brother Josh for introducing me to a Web site that has informed, entertained, addicted, and impoverished me for the last several years. The site is the Internet Movie Database, or IMDb.com, and if this column acts as an invitation to the uninitiated, I apologize.

Along with sports, reading, writing, and music, my favorite pastime is movies. By that, I refer to almost everything related to film. Watching movie discussion and review shows, reading about films and the "talent" associated with them, viewing classic clips on YouTube (my second and last plug of this column), arguing about films with friends and strangers, and occasionally even watching an actual movie.

It's curious to me that Josh turned me on to this site; he isn't exactly the biggest movie buff on the planet. I think that *The Shawshank Redemption, A League of Their Own,* and *My Cousin Vinny* are the last three movies he's seen. One masterpiece, and two amusing little flicks, and none of them released more recently than (let me double-check this on IMDb) 1994. We don't have too many discussions about movies (beyond those three and maybe those two old standbys, *Tootsie* and *Amadeus*—both now available on DVD by the way), not that it makes him a bad guy. Quite the contrary: he's bright as hell, works sixty hours on a slow week, and then takes pride in spending quality time with his wife and their four daughters.

My suspicion is that even if he could find the free time that I carve out, he wouldn't log anything approaching the chunks of time I do on IMDb—from fifteen minutes to multiple hours every single day. Some people, even those from the same gene pool, just don't have the knack of finding distractions like yours truly. But I digress.

Like most addictions, IMDb started as an innocuous little way to research facts about movies. In the old days, perhaps in the fifteen years prior to my addiction, whenever I used to watch movies at home, I would have one of those paperback movie guidebooks nearby, if said reference book wasn't hiding under the seat cushions with the potato chips, pens, watches, and remote controls. That five-hundred-page bible would tell me what that movie critic felt about a particular film (usually rating it from ½* to *****), its running time, year of release, and then list the director and maybe five cast members. Using this book was a little better than vainly asking, "Oh, what's her name ... wasn't she also in *The Treasure of the Whatchamacallit*"? With elusive bible in hand, I could say, "Oh, wait a second, wasn't she also in *The Treasure of the*...er, um...*Sierra Madre*? That's it, and, er, yeah, that may be her." You see, that sort of poking and hoping was state-of-the-art movie research back then.

With the advent of what has become my favorite Web site in the universe, I found myself now able to research all of the above information, plus discover and/or confirm every single cast member and character in every movie and TV show known to mankind. If I clicked a few more times, I could then find the filmographies, biographies, mythologies, and trivialities of anyone who ever appeared on a big or small screen. Yet, there was more, much more. Why not check out all the alluring photos of Raquel Welch, Ann-Margret, Rita Hayworth, and Roseanne Barr? Or how about seeing all of the awards that a film or actor/director was nominated for and won? The above is only a scratch of the surface of what this cyberhaven can do.

After awhile, I was happy to learn that my *wundersite* allowed me to discuss, scrutinize, praise, or rip apart any movie I decided to zero in on. My craze started innocently enough, and I found myself posting either a capsule or a feature-length review every week or so. What a great outlet! It beat trying to have a decent, animated discussion with my wife, family, friends, and colleagues. I consider only one of my friends, a self-described movie shut-in who sees about 150 new releases each year, a real movie buff; most are casual fans who don't get obsessed as I do about characters and story lines. They just don't see the beauty of spending precious hours and days pissed off that a key supporting character's back story was not developed enough for my liking. Go figure.

As I have gotten older, I've discovered that I tend to react even more emotionally to movies. If I have to define a quality that I most respond to in films, it is compelling human drama—whether delivered as straight drama, comedy, fantasy, or some combination of those genres. The main ingredient I gravitate to, other than great acting, is superior writing. A great screenwriter will show a love, or at least an understanding of, the characters presented and he/

she will also respect the audience's mind, heart, and conscience. Every now and then, a movie will be released to lavish critical praise—such as *21 Grams, Million Dollar Baby,* or the recent milkshake-thriller, *There Will Be Blood*—yet utterly fail to impress me. Not only that, but in the case of these three, the film will either so badly butcher the story, or present one-dimensional, buffoonish characters or so insult my intelligence by its total lack of subtlety that I will leave the theatre not only frustrated, but positively enraged. I'm a fairly level-headed guy, and I can think of only two other things that equally anger me: getting lost at two in the morning in or around New York City, or watching my Eagles blow another playoff game.

The beauty of the world's greatest Web site is that it has discussion boards for every single movie ever released. For a latent movie freak, this has mostly been a good thing. With IMDb as my outlet, I don't have quite as many conversations with colleagues and friends that go something like this:

Hey Jeff, have you seen any good movies recently?

Yeah, I've seen a couple.

Really? You didn't happen to see Million Dollar Baby, *did you?*

Yeah, my wife dragged me to see that, but it was pretty good.

You really liked that?

Yeah, it was kinda slow and depressing, but really deep. What did you think?

Man, Million Dollar Baby *evidently relied upon the most insulting screenplay I've ever had to sit through. The characters were totally one-dimensional and the film pretended to tackle serious issues, but did so in the most heavy-handed, intellectually dishonest way possible. And then you had the most underwritten characters I've ever seen with Maggie's buffoonish family, and don't even get me started on the Danger character. This movie pretended to stand for—*

Yo, Matt, I gotta go.

Wait; hold on, we didn't get to discuss the Blue Bear, and that lowest common denominator, jingoistic ...

For some reason, Jeff and I haven't discussed movies in the last few years. But who cares, when I can light up the discussion boards, and even get messages in my inbox every time someone replies to one of my brilliant posts? While it doesn't replace face-to-face human contact, it's much better in many respects. With IMDb, I don't have to make an effort to listen as much as I talk. Indeed, I'm not distracted by the yawns that I seem to inspire in others, and I don't have to worry about losing a friend with my industrial strength opinions.

Still, my gratitude to IMDb—the gateway to so much information, entertainment, and the first online message boards I've ever utilized—is tempered by the occasional reality check that I subject myself to. During these moments of harsh self-evaluation, I question the fact that I can shamelessly spend upward of two hours straight debating cinema among an international community of film scholars, students, dropouts, and fellow time-squanderers. My educated guess is that the average age of these denizens of the deep discussion is about half of mine.

I'm not sure if I like being one of the older residents of this community; in fact, I'm decidedly ambivalent about it. On the one hand, it's cool to hang with the younger folks, but on the other hand, it's depressing to find I'm attracted to the same discussions as what seem to be mostly seventeen-year-olds.

With your indulgence, in the next installment of "The Tip of the Goldberg," I will discuss the pleasures, pains, perils, and peeves of debating movies (and yes, even politics and all things semihuman) with people half my age on my favorite Web site of them all. See you then!

Still Semiaddicted After All These Years ...

April 2008

I have come to the stark realization that I possess some of the classical traits of an addictive personality. Shamelessly, I still pride myself on not being addicted to alcohol, drugs, gambling, womanizing, shopping, or shoplifting (please don't be misled by a previous column that talked about my abusing the term "guest services" in a local supermarket), as if that is some great virtue. But I realize that I am hopelessly addicted to anything that distracts me from the task at hand, and find any excuse to watch TV, surf online, discuss, watch and play sports, and engage in all sorts of other meaningless tasks that improve the quality of my life very marginally.

Occasionally, I am able to use my distractibility and powers of procrastination to my advantage. As a recent member of a Toastmasters chapter that meets on Monday evenings, I volunteered to give a five-to-seven-minute speech that I would presumably prepare for during the course of the preceding week. On Monday at 4:00 pm, with no topic or even an outline of an outline to guide me, I decided that there could be only one topic that I could talk about with some expertise—

procrastination. In the speech, I took about three minutes to get to a point—any point whatsoever—and then elaborated on why procrastination isn't always such a good strategy.

With apologies to Abraham Lincoln, it turned out to be a speech of, by, and for procrastinators. If he would've waited a little longer to address us at Gettysburg, he may have done the same. But enough of this tangent ...

... and back to my story. Several years ago, my brother Josh introduced me to a Web site that is the ultimate guide to everything related to movies and even TV shows. Last time, I mentioned how this Web site—IMDb.com—enabled me to research every monumental and trivial tidbit connected to films and also opened up a whole new world of reviewing and debating my favorite and least favorite films, actors, and directors with a fairly anonymous worldwide grouping of distractible people. Through the powers of deductive reasoning, I have also concluded that the average age of an IMDb-er is about half of mine, which if you'rc doing the math, makes me twice as old as them. This virtual fact has left me decidedly ambiguous.

As addictions go, this site has been stronger than chocolate chip mint ice cream or Vienna Wafers® and almost up there with watching the tube while eating ice cream and cookies. I now find myself availing myself of the discussion boards, open to anyone who takes enough time to complete the registration: Step One—come up with a user name; Step Two—come up with a password that you have some chance of remembering; Step Three—acknowledge that you read and understood the rules of usage, which you will never, ever read.

On an average day when I don't have any appointments that take me away from my home office, I'll venture to the discussion boards to see what's happening on a board called Oscar Buzz. Here, I'll weigh in on everything that has to do with who is going to be nominated and win the major awards. Fascinating, huh? Now as a movie buff, I usually see enough films to hang, yet I find the real regulars here tend to watch two hundred or more films a year, are in "university" overseas, and pretend to know every frame of every film by directors with names like Tarkovsky. I don't know whether to envy or pity them, though occasionally I learn something from the less obnoxious ones.

Occasionally within the same thread—I've learned that everything starts with the posting of a topic, and then all the replies to that post (Oscar Buzz may get one thousand or so posts a day, many of them at least somewhat literate) constitute a thread—I'll see much more incisive, intellectual commentary than you'll ever get from a Roger Ebert, in between strings of personal insults, vitriolic opinions and invective, and some of the most mindless mutterings I'll ever encounter outside of Fox News. (Apologies for that monstrosity of a sentence.)

The challenge for me in working this board is to not come off as too much of an authority and blow my cover, but to have the freedom of attacking movies, actors, and directors without attacking fans of the same. It's a line that I feel I can straddle well, but you'd be amazed at all the people who cannot debate passionately without insulting others in the process. Mentality-wise, they are the first cousins of those who cannot play sports competitively without being a lousy teammate or a downright horse's ass in the process. I commune with both of these types and pride myself on being neither. It doesn't pay the bills, but makes it easier to sleep when I'm not on IMDb battling insomnia for other reasons.

I also try to use humor irreverently, if not sarcastically, giving points of sorts to those who seem to get and, better yet, even advance the humor. There are some denizens of Oscar Buzz who post all day and night and adopt screen names of their favorite characters or actors and even change their names every few months or so, perhaps after they wear out their welcome with their old identities. They and others, to *broad-brush* it, will have signature phrases on the bottom of every post, usually quoting a great (to them) cinematic one-liner. For what it's worth, and to be honest, I also have a signature ready-to-go, a favorite weird line from an obscure poem of mine that reads "...sometimes childish adult world of anarchy, ruthlessness, and liverwurst." This curious line prefills on my reply screen, but I usually erase it. To be even more honest, the reason I don't use it very often is that nobody has had the curiosity and decency to ask me about it.

From Oscar Buzz, I have now found myself addicted to another board called Politics, which has me conversing with Marxists, Neo-Cons, cynics, zealots, and everyone in between. The discussion here is a little more aggressive as the longtime residents of this world really flex their keyboard muscles—hiding behind their anonymity to either try to prove their intellectual superiority or simply blast anyone who doesn't agree with them. I've been coming here for about four or five months, but have *met* some who have been here since its inception about ten years ago. The average age on this board seems to be in the thirties or so, as teens and WWII vets alike match philosophies, wits, and insults. I try to pick my spots here, avoiding like the plague anything having to do with racism, sexism, or any exclusionary–ism, but I jump in to debate policies, political punditry, and some philosophy. I post fairly often but try to stay under the radar enough to not be too recognizable.

Of course, Oscar Buzz, Politics, and the boards for various movies are not enough to satiate the posting appetite of someone of my semiaddictive nature and I must confess that I also have been spending some time on the *American Idol* board. What can I say? Outside of sports, movies, political shows, and news, this is the only show I watch, even though I know it has been rigged since I started watching it in season three. I post pretty aggressively there, unleashing more conspiracy theories than I ever do on the Politics board, and apparently both agreeing and butting heads with people who are younger than my average sweat sock.

There is so much more I can bore you with, but I'll leave you with something resembling a lesson. The biggest regret I have of wasting so much time and potential money-making opportunities on my cyberhaven is that I am feeding into one of the things that irk me the most about contemporary society and modern media. The lines between politicians, musicians, movie stars, and sports "heroes" is so blurred that everything just bleeds into the world of *celebrities.* I love the convenience of this site that lets me overanalyze *There Will Be Blood,* caustically criticize the media for their coverage of the Reverend Wright saga, and then opine about how off-key Jason Castro was while singing some mediocre Neil Diamond song—and I can do all this in about a ten-minute time frame. I put the same amount of passion and thought into each post, and into each topic, and that upsets me just a little. Maybe not as much as it would piss off my wife if she knew how much time I spent there but enough to cause me some insomnia, which in turn I work off by returning to IMDb.

All of my time on IMDb brings to mind the famous adage, "Be careful what you wish for," as this site has exceeded my wildest dreams as a one-stop shop for movie/TV research and quasi-social experiences. In defense of this site and myself, I find consolation in not being addicted to drugs, alcohol, or the theft of women's hair scrunchies, and in the parlance of discussion boards, I never do any of the following—which may be topics for another column:

- Troll—or start a false thread just to get people upset
- Flame—just unload invective on some poor unsuspecting shlemiel
- Use computer abbreviations, such as "lol"; shoot me if I ever do that
- Use those flashing little emoticons; hurt me if I ever use those
- Pretend to represent movie stars, movie studios, or politicians; I only represent my own opinions and I try to say the same things I would if face-to-face
- Maintain my anonymity—not revealing my true name, picture, and much of my personal life as many others do without a second thought

All this may excuse the fact that I am semiaddicted to things in life that won't make me rich, famous, or as much of an asset to society as I may have imagined, but I do have my dignity. Who can put a price on that?

What's in a Name?

June 2008

What if Attila the Hun were named Timmy the Hun? Would he have been less barbaric and bloodthirsty, and would fifth-century life—such as we know about it—have been any more peaceful?

I find myself asking such questions while preparing to become a first-time dad; the due date is projected to be July 22. It's an exciting time for my wife and me, although in many respects the thought of doing so well into my forties gives me a lot of *agita*. The good news is that I may have matured a little since graduating from my physical prime and my wife, both younger and smarter than me, has been feeling great. So all signs, should we continue to be blessed, herald a relatively easy pregnancy for Ruby and a beautiful baby to enter our lives within the next couple of months. Everything else is secondary, yet of all the secondary issues, the paramount question is, "So what are we going to name him?"

Okay, we gave in to temptation and technology and found out that we are having a boy. Some debate preceded that decision, but I think that we made the right call there; if the ultrasound tech and doctor saw what they thought they saw, I think it was the right decision. With that key information in place, we have spent the last six weeks or so batting around some possible names, but it's been more an informal process than a concerted effort to reach a final verdict.

As of now, we have his last name and his middle name locked in. The last name was a choice between Goldberg, Tan-Goldberg (my wife, honoring her tradition, held onto her maiden name), and Tanberg—the latter being the informal last name of our dearly departed cocker spaniel. Without any real debate, we went with Goldberg. His middle name will be Jun, pronounced more like *gin* than *June*, which is a tribute to the first names of Ruby's own parents. If you're scoring at home, our beautiful baby boy's name will be ___ Jun Goldberg, or "Blank" Jun Goldberg. For the last few months, we have referred to him as *BJG*—a designation that may or may not expire sometime around July 22, 2008.

How do we go about filling in the blank? Having picked out the middle name, Ruby has been very generous in giving me the lion's share of the responsibility of naming our baby, although I willingly concede to her full veto power. Like most other couples facing this awesome challenge, we have done just a little bit of research while also considering the following eight factors. (We have not yet consulted a magic eight-ball, but that may be the arbiter of choice if Ruby enters the maternity ward with nothing more than *BJG* to put on the birth certificate.)

1. Family Names—As I understand Jewish tradition, a newborn is not to be named after the living. While I love my family, I was not *that* close to either of my grandfathers, and their names also don't do that much for me—Joseph on my dad's side and Hyman on my mom's. Dad did not have any brothers, and I did not get to know Mom's brothers (Albert, Charlie, and Issie) all that well. The best opportunity for a family tribute would be to honor my mother of loving memory—Sara. There is no tailor-made male counterpart for that name, but one of the names we have considered is Samuel—which is in the same neighborhood. It's certainly in our top five or ten at this point.

2. Friends—I have been blessed with some good, close friends over the years, but I don't know if I want to name my baby after one of them. It's a gray area to be sure, even though my best friend in college and in life, David, named his first son Matthew. I've never known if he was named after me, per se, though I am honored (and it also scares me a little) that Matt—a terrific kid—just graduated college. My erstwhile roommate and I have no secret blood oath to name our first offspring after one another, but I do like his name, as I like other names of good friends, including Jeffrey, Steve(n), and Michael. Having said that, Ruby has apparently vetoed all of these suggestions.

3. Nicknames—One always has to consider the nicknames, official or otherwise, that a kid will be subject to. Of course, one can't predict whether he will be called "'Stretch" or "Four-Eyes" or "Dumbass," but a little careful planning can avoid your gift to the world being called Dick—not that there's anything (necessarily) wrong with that.

4. The Unisex Factor—Perhaps, it's another hang-up of mine, but I am trying to avoid all unisex names, such as Robin or Chris or Taylor (none were on my short list, anyway.) Our delightful three-year-old nephew's name is Alexander, and he's just now being called Alex on occasion. I should not be concerned that "Alex" seems to be more the province of girls these days, but I am.

Then again, the shortened form of Samuel is Sam, and women's bathrooms seem to be populated with a lot of Sams as well as Alexes. All this makes me very confused, yet I am firm in my resolve not to name our son Emily.

5. Rhyme with Body Parts?—Enos is a fine biblical name that apparently means "man." But, let's face it: on my watch, my son will not be named Enos nor will he answer to Ripple or Huttocks. He will thank me later for my apparent immaturity.

6. Commonality Versus Uniqueness—This is a tough category for me as I really don't want the consideration of the popularity of names to dissuade me from an otherwise good choice. Looking at a list of the ten most popular baby names in 2007 (my crack research team couldn't find a 2008 list), three of those spots were held by the given names of my brothers and me. Ruby and I are also not overly enamored with the rest of the top ten, so we should be okay here.

By the same token, I also don't want to follow in the footsteps of celebs like Frank Zappa and Gwyneth Paltrow who named their kids Moon Unit and Apple, respectively. I may broaden this category to rule out the twenty most common names of 2007 on the one side of the equation, and all astronomical terms and fruit on the other.

7. Astrology—Well, sort of. Ruby and I are both Leos, and *BJG,* if he hangs in there another day or so past his ETA, will join our little zodiac club. Ruby has proposed that if we are still undecided about his name and his birth date is July 23 or later, we should name him Leo. I'm lukewarm to this idea and will appropriate veto power if necessary. Stay tuned.

8. Initials, Etc.—With his middle name (Jun) in place, there is no chance that our son's initials will spell trouble for him. Imagine if his name was **P**eter **I**an **G**oldberg; that may be asking for trouble from the various wiseasses he will surely encounter. In fact, I defy any of them to spell out a word with a "J" in the middle—the same letter that is in the middle of the initials for my dad (RJG) and for me (MJG). In both cases, the "J" is for Joseph, my grandfather's name.

With respect to initials, I've also gotten quite attached to *BJG*—it just sounds kind of cool to me. But do we force in a "B" name just to validate a cute pre-natal nickname? Or do we avoid a good "B" name—Benjamin, Bruce, Barry—just to avoid that consideration?

Questions such as the above never stop as our quest continues to give our boy the type of cool, not too popular, not too unique, meaningful first name that will give him a strong connection to his families, a clear identity, and no urgency to fight the neighborhood bullies. As we don't know for certain when the delivery date will be, I am in the process of suggesting to Ruby that we decide on his first name by July 4. Truth be told, the Leo-by-default strategy is scaring me just a little, my implicit veto power notwithstanding.

So, in the meantime, I will continue to ponder enough unanswerable questions about the likes of Attila the Hun to inform this decision. For instance: what about Woody Allen, one of my favorite writers and directors? That first name is too identifiable with a certain body part, and what influence did that have over his predatory dating habits? And then there's Orenthal James Simpson, as great a running back as I've ever seen, but, well, his story did not end there.

In many ways, the naming process is just beginning, but we're going to get this right. And then, we'll just have three little things to worry about:

1) His traditional Chinese name
2) His traditional Hebrew name
3) Oh yeah, the small details of feeding him, wiping him, raising him, loving him, and giving him every chance of leading a beautiful life.

Can Every Day Be Father's Day?

July 2008

As I am writing this, it is eight days past Father's Day 2008, and eight days closer to my very first such occasion as a father of a human being. For the purpose of this column, I am not counting my all-too-brief six years as the proud father of the most lovable cocker spaniel ever to be unleashed upon this world.

This annual day for fathers was spent with my usually radiant, almost-ready-to-deliver wife Ruby, her mom, one of my brothers and his eternal fiancée, and, of course, my dad. My other brother connected with us by phone from Israel, and the rather enjoyable day was spent in our usual fashion—sharing a little personal news, some political discussion, more wisecracking and puns, and my taking advantage of the festive occasion by eating like a sumo wrestler in training.

Father's Day Weekend 2008 started with the shocking news that NBC political news giant Tim Russert had suddenly passed. The timing of his all-too-early departure seemed fitting, as Russert was widely respected for his professional greatness and admired and beloved even more for the way in which he adored his family—especially his son and his father. Even after the veteran NBC newsman achieved the unofficial status as most respected political pundit and interviewer in the country, he retained his reverence for his father, "Big Russ" to him, a decidedly unglamorous, hard-working, and soft-spoken man from Buffalo.

Indeed, it is my own dad, a career journalist from the equally balmy city of St. Paul, Minnesota, who has always enjoyed political discussion shows, including *Meet The Press*, a prestigious show that Tim Russert brought to an even higher level. While I still enjoy watching these shows, I rarely take the opportunity to watch them with Dad, and my experience is all the poorer for it.

As I view these programs, I miss Dad's level of political awareness, his advocacy for fairness—especially as the concept relates to workers' rights and civil rights—along with his wit. Dad's wit, sharpened by his mastery of the English language, is often employed against those he finds to be *blowhards* or *four flushers*, two of his favorite terms of nonendearment over the years. Unlike my own sense of humor, Dad's is rarely profane, and it almost never is used to call attention to him. The beauty of it—an expression he may use, but (typically) never to confer credit or praise upon himself—is that his wit can inform the moment without him ever coming off as a wiseguy. Maybe this has something to do with the time and place of his birth, a 1925 winter's day in the modest, but capital, city of St. Paul.

The limitations of this space and my own writing ability will not allow me to do much justice to my thoughts about fatherhood and about Dad, but let me take a quick shot at it. I am thankful that Dad lives within about seven miles of us, even as I sometimes give in to profound sadness over the circumstances in which he lives. For the last almost six years, since Mom also departed much too soon, he has lived (by his choice) in a continuing care retirement facility called the Evergreens. Within the Evergreens, he lived independently in a single apartment for almost three years, and adjusted rather well to the smaller space and the much more communal style of living—a somewhat dramatic change from the house he had lived in for forty years, an average-sized dwelling that few people outside of immediate family were wont to visit.

Dad, who never thought of himself as a real social animal, soon befriended most of his neighbors and took part in a variety of organized activities ranging from tai chi, to bowling, to current events, to a religious discussion group with the facility's chaplain. In his spare time, he would regularly trounce (without boasting) a group of residents/friends at Scrabble, cook himself one presumably tasty and healthful soup-type concoction a day, do his sit-ups in the morning and push-ups at night, and frequently take three-mile walks to the local grocery store, filling a knapsack with mostly canned goods. He loved to spend his spare, spare time with family—getting together when we could and talking on the phone when we couldn't. His eyesight, never all that good even when it was good, had now deteriorated to the point where it was too much of an effort for him to drive or even to read, an activity that brought this voracious reader and learner much pleasure, perspective, and wisdom.

Never one to waste much time on TV (unlike his wife and his youngest son who is writing now with the TV blaring a tennis match in the background), he caught up on the news by listening (the experience more meaningful when his hearing aids were adjusted) to CNN and sharing the newspaper in the morning with his across-the-hall neighbor. Dad bought her a subscription to *The Philadelphia Inquirer*, a paper he helped edit for thirty-four years, and would walk down three flights of stairs to get it and bring it to her. In return, his good friend would read the headlines and main stories to him over breakfast.

Sometime within those first three years, I began a tradition of reading the Sunday comic strips with him, especially reading him *Prince Valiant,* a saga he has followed closely for most of his eighty-three years. While I was never a fan of the strip, reading *Prince Valiant* has become a cherished part of our routine and an excuse of sorts to get together at least once a week, usually on the weekend. And I never start reading until Dad starts with "Our Story," the opening bell to Val's adventure, before we segue to some of his other favorites, like *Beetle Bailey, The Lockhorns* (used to be better twenty years ago, by the way), *Cathy, Hagar the Horrible,* and *The Piranha Club.*

Three and a half years ago, Dad suffered a stroke, mostly from complications of a supposedly routine liver biopsy. With some help, he fought the good fight, his inherent optimism and appreciative nature allowing him to almost never give in to despair. After a couple of weeks in the hospital, he resided in the skilled nursing unit of the Evergreens, sharing a room and a bathroom with a man who always seemed (as Dad would describe it) to be using said bathroom when nature was calling my dad to the throne.

Six months after this event, he has battled back to where he is now, in a private room in the assisted living section. Although his cane-assisted walk is somewhat unsteady, and his eyesight next to nil, he takes part in most of the activities offered, regularly trouncing (matter-of-factly) his fellow residents in Trivial Pursuit, taking part in discussions with the chaplain, and attending musical programs, his favorites being sing-a-longs where in his (never great when it was great) spirited baritone, he will absolutely nail the lyrics to most of the songs played. Perhaps I'm not quite as objective as Dad, but my sadness over the limitations of his current lifestyle is somewhat mitigated by what I observe at the Evergreens—staff, residents, and their family members have all come to know and truly appreciate Dad for what he has always been—intelligent, thoughtful, considerate, and appreciative of what he has and what he receives from others.

Typically at around 7:30 pm each evening, just before Dad's bedtime (even when Dad stayed up late, he would never stay up *late),* I look forward to our evening phone conversations. Usually, one of us will pull the trigger and ask the other about his day, or in the rare event one of us feels we have any *real* news to share, lead off the conversation with that tidbit.

We'll discuss family, politics, and current events, and then steer into other areas, which may include family memories, the evening's Final Jeopardy! answer, samples from a book of quotes, a riddle that Dad may have just coined, Minnesota talk and nostalgia, or sometimes he will ask me if I ever heard a particular song (and even if I had, I will say "no.") He will then commence to regale me, and often in the middle of the third or so verse, stop himself and say, "Ooh, that must be terrible to listen to." Suffice it to say that it ain't Sinatra or Nat King Cole, but I hope to hear several thousand more renditions from him.

Before hanging up, my Dad will always conclude with some variation on "Well, thank you for the call, I enjoyed it, and may the Holy One, blessed be He, bless you, Ruby, Ruby's *mishpocha,* and the baby with a good evening. Good night." Coming from this intelligent, warm, modest, and not overly religious man whom I love dearly, I am touched by this sincere coda every single time.

Sometime later in July, should he be on time, my own son, "(Blank) Jun Goldberg" (or BJG, as currently referred to by Ruby and me) will enter this world. I know that I will be an older, yet somehow younger, father than Dad was to me, and I hope that I will be half the father that my dad was in so many profound ways. If characteristics skip a generation, I will be proud if/when BJG becomes a very bright, considerate, witty, sincere person with a great appreciation for other people and cultures, and a lifelong zest for learning.

Better yet, I look forward to the moment when Ruby and I can present BJG for his new grandfather to hold, kiss, and touch with his innate goodness. I daydream about all the moments that they will share and pray that my dad will be healthy enough to directly help to shape my son's life.

This usually irreverent writer (sorry) can picture it now. BJG is sitting on my dad's lap, and after hearing "Our Story," launches into the adventures of Prince Valiant and the interesting characters he encounters, battles, and saves. His eyes and his voice dance with the true joy of the moment: he is reading aloud, enjoying an exciting strip that has been around for about one thousand years, and sharing all this with his beloved "Grandpa," or the less generic nickname he has for him. Perhaps my dad will sing to him in that deep, almost on-key voice, or maybe my son will join him in a duet, with or without my warbling.

On this extended Father's Day season, and with as much of Dad's sincerity and as much of Mom's creative sentimentality as I can muster and share with you, I pray to the Holy One, blessed be He, for this moment.

What America Means to Me

A Short Essay for the July 2008 Issue

As July 4 approaches, and we collectively mark our 232nd anniversary (my, how time flies), it is time for some celebration and reflection.

Being an American is one part of my identity, one that I have largely taken for granted. While I am indebted to so many—from our founding fathers to those who have given their lives in battle for me to enjoy freedoms that I mostly accept as a given—I still don't know how truly patriotic I am.

To me, being an American is about expressing our inalienable rights to make our nation and our world a better place. It is about not only tolerating and accepting but also embracing people, cultures, and ideas that may be different from my own. It is about living up to the ideals expressed in the Declaration of Independence and formalized within our remarkable Constitution—especially the Preamble, which talks about forming a more perfect union.

Being an American means that I am often at odds with the decisions of our government, yet I know that America gives me that very freedom to debate and dissent. It is about the recognition that I will be disappointed at times, precisely because our promise is so great and our standards are so high. My American identity also guarantees that many around the world will be both jealous of our freedoms and derisive of our power, and our sometimes superior attitude.

Being an American sometimes means that I am embarrassed by the crassness and commercialization of almost everything from our holidays to our politics. It is the uncomfortable realization that many of us are more divisive than unifying in our attitudes toward others that may look different, speak a different native language, or pray in a way that is foreign to us.

But for all of our flaws and for all of the work we need to do to live up to our promise, I still rejoice in this beautiful land, in our great achievements and in our cultural icons that comprise Americana. There are so many places I long to see right here at home—from Mt. Rushmore, to Yellowstone, to the Big Sky Country, to the Grand Canyon. I will never get tired of nor lose my reverence for the Statue of Liberty and Ellis Island, beacons of freedom to so many who did not have my luxury of taking our liberties for granted.

My heart will still swell with pride when I salute the flag, and with it every ideal and everybody that it represents. And whether I enjoy the fireworks display at my local high school football stadium, my neighboring city of Philadelphia (where it all began, in so many ways), or watch one of the broadcasts on TV, I long to hear the stirring musical soundtrack of our nation. And please don't blame me if I tear up every time I hear Ray Charles sing *America the Beautiful.*

The Circus is Coming to Town

August 2008

A few months ago, my wife Ruby asked me if I knew the answer to a riddle that goes something like this. What are the three rings associated with marriage? The answer, I have learned, is: the engagement ring, the wedding ring, and the suffer*ing*. Presumably, the author of this riddle forgot about such rings as the boxing ring, whimper*ing*, and surrender*ing,* although he/she did seem to acknowledge that married life resembles a three-ring circus.

As I write, today is Ruby's due date, and I'm sitting in the waiting room. No, not *that* waiting room. I'm in the *green room* of my car dealership, waiting for my turn signal to be fixed. Our son to be, (Blank) Jun Goldberg, or BJG, is still holding out for the perfect moment to drop into position and we are waiting to bestow the perfect first name upon him. All this has me thinking: If married life is a three-ring circus, how many rings are associated with being a first-time dad?

With a nod to the Summer Olympics opening in Beijing on 8-8-08, I thought that I would write about the multiringed circus of fatherhood. Just as the Olympics logo has five rings (which as we all know stand for cheating, misplaced nationalism, blood doping, steroids, and biased officiating), my initial impulse was to match that number. But after ruminating on this for an additional few minutes in the most idealistic Olympic spirit (sincere amateurism), I realized that limiting this exercise to just five rings would not earn me any medals.

I now present, in alphabetical order, the twenty-five rings of fatherhood, "The Tip of the Goldberg"-style. If you're scoring at home, that's enough for two decathlons with a modern pentathlon thrown in for good measure.

The Twenty-Five Ring Circus of Fatherhood

1. Aspir*ing*—Much as I'm *perspiring* thinking about all of this, I'm aspiring to be a good dad, and hopefully I will play a part in *inspiring* BJG's own aspirations, whatever they may turn out to be. The trick will be balancing my own aspirations with my son's, and knowing when to yield the right of way to him.

2. Bewilde*ring*—While I have had many years and the better part of nine months to prepare for this, it is still a bit surreal that I will be holding our own beautiful baby in just a few days. So what is the source of my bewilderment? Have I wanted to be a father for a long time? Yes. Do I love my wife? Absolutely. Do I think she'll be a good mom? Certainly. So there's no reason to feel overwhelmed, right? Wrong.

3. Cate*ring*—We're talking about a boy born into a Chinese/Jewish household here. It's all about the food, right? We're planning a small ceremony for his bris (talk about *suffering* in the name of modern medical science and good old-fashioned Jewish ritual) and I think we'll do the food spread ourselves. Here's the basic agenda: 1) greet the rabbi/cantor; 2) say a few blessings; 3) attempt to avert our eyes from the circumcision itself; 4) down a drink or two; 5) grab some bagels and lox; 6) add some *schmeer*; 7) enjoy a fattening dessert or two; and 8) repeat steps 4–7 and make a day of it.

4. Diape*ring*—Okay, I've watched many a diaper being changed and I used to pick up my cocker spaniel's number two (and even count the pieces at times), but this is a whole new ballgame. I did take a five-minute lesson as part of a new daddy workshop, but I'm *shvitzing* again just thinking about it. I'm not too eager to mess up the clean-up, so maybe the better d-word should be *deferring*.

5. Explo*ring*—Nothing excites me more than musing about all the exploring that BJG's going to do and how the world will start to renew itself through his young eyes.

6. Filibuste*ring*—Here's my choice: fill a diaper, or filibuster?

7. Glowe*ring*—I'm *picturing* Ruby's reaction as I'm *butchering* the *diapering* or doing too much *filibustering*.

8. Hampe*ring*—As in, "This baby's hampering our sleep habits." Or hampering could be the practice of throwing all the dirty clothes in the container for another day's *laundering*.

9. Interfe*ring*—Let me explain. My mother-in-law, who I otherwise love, is living with us. At times, I'm not sure who's interfering with whom around here.

10. Jee*ring*—I imagine that a crowd is watching me as I prepare to put my son safely into his car seat. Still a little shaken from my practice round, I succumb to the pressure, take way too long, and even wrap the seatbelt around my middle finger. The crowd, a typical Philadelphia sports mob, lives up to its reputation and boos me with gusto.

11. Koshe*ring*—Okay, we don't intend to start keeping a kosher home (too many great Chinese recipes that don't qualify), but we will make an effort to get the house just a little more kosher for the bris. As the Talmud says, "It's better to be koshering than *Yom Kippuring.*"

12. Linge*ring*—I know that everything will go smoothly, yet there are still some lingering doubts about my being a good father. The doubts have been around for so long that I think they're becoming *loitering* doubts.

13. Misfi*ring*—Hey, even the best marksmen learn toilet training by trial and error.

14. Numbe*ring*—All the numbers, including his number one and number two—but not only those. We look forward to numbering his first burp, his first steps, his first words, his first everything.

15. Outsource*ring*—Should be a word. When nurturing our offspring becomes too overpowering a task, we'll occasionally outsource the work to my dear aforementioned mother-in-law.

16. Pande*ring*—Works in politics, right? Hopefully, as BJG grows, we'll be able to somewhat minimize our level of *pampering* and *pandering* to his every want. Stay tuned.

17. Quive*ring*—with anticipation, with excitement, with jitters, with extra pounds.

18. Raptu*ring*—Or is it rupturing? As in what will be happening to the discs in my lower back from carrying him around day after day?

19. Smatte*ring*—That's the amount of sleep we can look forward to in the foreseeable future. Honorable mentions go to *slobbering, soldiering,* and *surrendering. Suffering* is purely optional, and not part of my present baby vocabulary.

20. Ti*ring*— I hope to never get tired of watching, hugging, kissing, feeding, playing with, and reading to him. It's just some of that other stuff that may get a little tiresome.

21. Unwave*ring*—My love for my wife and my son and my determination to retain what's left of my sanity.

22. Voluntee*ring*—What I'll soon find myself doing in regard to the *diapering* and *laundering,* to make myself just a little more useful and just a little less exasperating to Ruby. What a guy.

23. Wonde*ring*—How do billions of people seem to be able to do all this stuff so effortlessly, and I'm already a basket case? Just wondering.

24. Yamme*ring*—I wish I could promise not to become one of those parents who is constantly yammering about every little miracle that his little one performs.

Nobody needs to hear every single, sickening detail and I won't fall into that trap. Wanna lay odds?

25. Zoo-Ente-*ring*—What, you were expecting *"zippering?"* I can't wait till my son begs us to take him to the zoo, thus giving me an excuse to go there again. Of course, the zoo will be right here in our home for the next millennium or so.

Well, there you have it. More than twenty-five *rings* lie ahead for us as we await the appearance of BJG. The circus of life is renewing, and thankfully, it's coming to our home.

Ben There, Done All That?

September 2008

All About the Benjamins, billed as an action-comedy about how the pursuit of money makes us do some crazy things, hit the silver screens in March 2002. Its estimated budget was $14 million, or to use the slang, 140,000 Benjamins. Apparently, it wasn't a blockbuster smash, although its reception was a little warmer than, say, Ice Cube, who happened to be its star and co-writer. Yours truly has not spent a penny —let alone a *Benny*—to see it, and why should I? With that lethal combination of memories and Wikipedia going for me, I know quite a bit about a lot of Benjamins.

First, there's Benjamin Franklin, the reason why the $100 bill is called a Benjamin. More than two hundred years since his passing, I doubt that our country has ever produced anyone quite so fascinating and with so many achievements and identities, including those of statesman, diplomat, printer, writer, civic activist, philosopher, scientist, inventor, school dropout, runaway, musical composer, bon vivant, and visionary. His ideas and innovations would include the very first public libraries and fire departments, and his inventions comprised everything from the lighting rod and the glass harmonica to the Franklin stove and the urinary catheter. For good measure, he invented bifocals. Oh, and he still rose early enough to pen a truckload of sayings, teaching us about the thirteen virtues. And yes, his sense of smell was keen enough to warn us that "Fish and visitors stink after three days." This brilliant Renaissance man-about-town has probably had more national cities, buildings, warships, landmarks, and bridges named after him than any other American. When it comes to Bens, he'd have to be at the top of everyone's lists. Remember: A Benny saved ...

And then there's Benjamin Jeremy (Ben) Stein, a very bright man—and he'd be the first to admit it—who has droned his way into our consciousness as an attorney, former speechwriter for Nixon, a game show host, and a monotonous pitchman and actor. I admit to never really getting him or his politics. Furthermore, as a Nixon loyalist, it seems he has no love lost for another Ben, legendary *Washington Post* newsman Ben Bradlee, who helped pave the way for Nixon's political demise. *All The President's Ben(s)?*

Do you want a true presidential Ben? Look no further than Benjamin Harrison, our twenty-third president and grandson of William Henry (Tippecanoe) Harrison. Ben served one term and was the only prez to be preceded and succeeded by the same man, Grover Cleveland. Little Benny Harrison, celebrated in Indiana as the only Hoosier president, did serve all four years, which logged him about forty-seven more months in the Oval Office than his poor grandpa. By the way, Gramps delivered the longest ever inauguration speech before dying of pneumonia thirty days later. Tippecanoe's ratio of speech minutes per days in office is never likely to be topped. Well, we all have our distinctions in life—and death.

Before leaving the political arena, how about those noted Israeli Bens? There's Benjamin Netanyahu,

Israel's ninth prime minister, who held that office over ten years ago. Although born in the newly independent state of Israel, "Bibi" actually went to high school in the U.S. More specifically, he graduated from Cheltenham (Pennsylvania) High School three years after his brother, Yoni.

Yoni, an elite Israeli officer who lost his life while leading the heroic Operation Entebbe mission, also graduated high school with Mr. October, Reggie Jackson. For the record, Cheltenham High is about ten miles northeast of the Benjamin Franklin Bridge. Now, if an Israeli prime minister linked to a bridge doesn't satisfy your yen for political Bens, what about another former Prime Minister who has the country's busiest airport named after him—David Ben Gurion.

Okay, you've had enough of the Israeli Benjamins? How about *Disraeli*, Benjamin—a prolific author who happened to serve two terms as prime minister of Great Britain, the only Jewish man to ever hold that office. Although I did some kind of last-minute research paper on Disraeli in high school, I did not remember that the following quote was his. "There are three kinds of lies: lies, damn lies, and statistics." I would agree with that about 63 percent of the time. Honestly.

Not impressed with the Bens of modern history? Let's go back more than five thousand years pre-Franklin and head straight to the Bible, where we'll find a Benjamin so famous that he was simply known as, um, *Benjamin*. You know, like Cher or Madonna, but with a more pleasant singing voice. As the youngest of the twelve children of his aging father, Jacob (nearing one hundred when he was sired), Joseph's only younger brother was often referred to as Benny, or sometimes Benji. Baby Bro hated the latter nickname, explaining that it made him sound too preppy. (If he was embarrassed by being called Benji, he should've been thankful that he never had to wear his brother's amazing Technicolor dreamcoat.)

The world of entertainment would be much poorer were it not for the contributions of scores of Bens, including but not limited to Kingsley, who gave one of the best ever biopic performances in the title role of Gandhi. Then there's the sporadically funny Ben Stiller, who inherited great comedic bloodlines from his parents, Stiller and Meara. Ben's okay, but wake me up when he does anything as funny as his father's Frank Costanza, the man who celebrates Festivus but never removes his shoes in public. Still need more comedy? We have one of the old school kings of comedy, Benny Kubelsky, much better known as Jack Benny. Benny is eternally thirty-nine, still trying to play the right notes on his beloved violin and still thinking over his response when asked what should have been a no-brainer by the thug pointing a gun at his head—"Your money or your life?" Yep, Benny's still thinking it over.

So you like your comedy a little wilder and shamelessly burlesque? I defy you to find a funnier show than the one presided over by the late, great Alfred Hawthorne (Benny) Hill. You like the more fictional TV characters? You can always watch reruns of *Bonanza*, featuring Ben Cartwright, macho patriarch of a prominent Virginia City family, and *Gentle Ben*, a sweet-natured bear and best friend to a young boy who traveled around the Florida swamps with his dad in an airboat. It seemed pretty cool at the time, although it's been a hundred years since I, or anyone else, has seen that little show.

When pronounced with a certain inflection, the term *ben-ben* means "running fast" in Mandarin. This term would seem to be apt to describe former

Canadian sprinter Ben Johnson who shocked the world at the 1988 Olympics. Ben-Ben smashed the world record, covering the distance in an astounding 9.79 seconds, defeating the great Carl Lewis in the process. His celebration was short-lived as he was subsequently disqualified for illegal doping. His popularity plummeted just as fast as he ran.

Not to worry, as there are always more Bens to go around. I haven't even mentioned Vereen and Affleck, golfers Hogan and Crenshaw, and then there's that Bernanke guy who heads the Federal Reserve Board. What about the kindly baby doctor, Dr. Benjamin Spock, infamous traitor Benedict Arnold and the anything but ben-evolent Il Duce, Benito Mussolini. Hey, I'd have to pop a *bennie* to help me stay up and write about all the Benjamins that are running though my head right now.

As I prepare to call off this brainstorm, my own little Ben—Benjamin Jun Goldberg, who is named after no Ben in particular—is rocking most comfortably in Grandma's arms. Benny, who I'm delighted to report is as healthy and happy as a twenty-four-day-old baby should be, just got fed the old-fashioned way by his mom. He showed his appreciation for his sustenance by letting out two world class burps. In this new world we are living in, Mom, Dad, and Grandma are deliriously happy with this development.

But I haven't lost my perspective on all this. As events go, I realize that it was one giant burp for Ben, if only one small burp for Ben-kind.

Identity Crisis?

October 2008

It's a rainy, blurry Saturday morning in Jersey and prior to watching yet more TV— including reliving the Presidential debate, listening to additional spin about the financial bailout, tuning into the baseball playoff races, catching a tribute or two to the late, great Paul Newman (wasn't he eternally cool and perennially about thirty years old?), and immersing myself in a little college football—I thought I'd try to find a little time before deadline to identify and analyze some of my identities. Don't worry; the previous should be the longest sentence of this column.

If someone were to ask me who/what I am, I'm not sure where I'd start. While it's too late to simulate a word association drill with myself, I'd probably think and say most of the following, in some order:

- Husband
- Father
- Jew
- American
- Sports Lover/Philly sports fan
- Democrat
- Writer

- (Whatever else I have done to make a living has never really been part of my "identity," which may be problematic, but that's for another time and venue.)

There are other identities based on personality attributes and the like; indeed, I am a slightly overweight, yet hyperkinetic, humorous, kind, open-minded, American Jewish Democratic husband-father-writer. With all of these identities, I really don't have an identity crisis in the normal sense of the expression. The problem is *not* that I'm confused about my identities. To be more accurate, my internal crises have been caused by my very awareness of the groups that I have always identified myself with. Let me try to explain.

Because of the tense presidential campaign and the convergence of the end of baseball and the start of football, I've been thinking especially about two of my identities—Philly sports fan and Democrat. For the last almost forty years I've accepted, if not celebrated, both of these identities as if they were as immutable as birthrights. In truth, I have full freedom of choice to leave both of these identities behind, but that is much easier said than done. Part of me thinks it wouldn't be so bad to do so. Forgetting about politics—and partisan presidential politics in particular—would free up a whole lot of time and energy for ... for ... something more valuable.

And what if I devoted less time, energy, and money toward following my Phillies, Eagles, Sixers, and Flyers? Wouldn't I benefit from more precious time, more and better sleep, and even some extra cash to dedicate to other passions? Furthermore, on balance, my Democrats and my Philly teams have lost a lot more contests than they have won under my passionate watch. So what gives—or why does nothing give?

When I was five years old, the 1964 edition of my hometown Philadelphia Phillies shocked the baseball world by getting off to an almost insurmountable lead in the National League pennant race. Well, it would've been insurmountable if this good fortune wasn't met by an unprecedented collapse, as the Phils lost ten straight games to give away the pennant. While I was too young to watch them at the time, this *"el choko"* is still part of the almost palpable Philadelphia *sportslore* and losers' complex that we all carry with us as baggage. Other towns have lovable losers that break our hearts but endear themselves to us; Philly teams kick us in the gut on a fortunate day, and deliver their blows to lower regions on a typical day.

In that same year, I faintly remember some Democrat named LBJ defeating some guy named Goldwater (I was young enough to wonder why the Gold**bergs** weren't fans of Gold**water**, but we were a Democratic family). They called it a landslide and I still remember asking what that was. To our way of thinking, the 1964 election was a case where the good guys won; the good guys comprised the party that helped the little guy, yearned for peace and worked to eliminate other injustices such as racial segregation. In the next few years as I kind of came of age, the world started becoming a little more confusing as we kept hearing reports of casualties from Vietnam, civil rights movements, peace protests, political assassinations, and other unrest. But my Democratic Party seal was stamped on my consciousness, as it continued to be the party that represented racial equality, peace, and unions versus corporations. They were also the people making cool movies and music and, incidentally, they seemed to have the hotter girls.

The sports world really hooked me from about 1966 on, when I started to memorize statistics while learning some of the finer points of the games. From age seven or so, I derived equal pleasure from playing and watching sports, and both of these passions have never waned. As my wife can joylessly aver, I can watch almost any sport being played at any level, from ice skating to cliff diving, but reserve my greatest passion for the four *major* team sports played—with whatever level of proficiency—by my Philadelphia sports teams. Despite all the losses these teams have racked up, we've had all-time great players (Julius Erving, Mike Schmidt, Bobby Clarke, Reggie White) and all-time great personalities (Charles Barkley, Allen Iverson, Buddy Ryan) and some great wins as well. Being a Philly sports fan has allowed me to break the ice in countless conversations, even if those from other cities assumed from my identity that I was a raving sociopath with a hockey puck for a brain.

Starting with a very close 1968 election that the other team (the dreaded Republicans) won, my team has won only three out of ten elections. As a voter, my record is a slightly better three for eight. I almost voted for an Independent in 1980, but in the end, couldn't resist voting for my team, which was on the wrong side in one of those infamous landslides, a GOP runaway. In fact, of those aforementioned seven defeats, five of them would be considered to be landslides; of *my* three wins, all of them were much too close to attain landslide status. But compared to my record as a Philly sports fan, I've kicked butt in presidential politics.

Sure, my sports teams have given me great moments and ice-breaking topics of conversation, but where are the championships? My baseball team was the first major sports franchise to amass ten thousand losses in its dubious history. The last of the four teams to win a championship was the Dr. J-led Sixers of 1983. For those scoring at home, that means that twenty-five years and one hundred combined seasons have passed since that day when I watched the game from a small room in Indianapolis. If memory serves, I was icing my ankle at the time (I had sprained it playing hoops at the JCC, no doubt tripping over the foot of a Republican) in a bucket and watching it on a twelve-inch, black-and-white number that was horizontal-hold challenged.

As October approaches, my Phillies will be in the playoffs, trying to win a World Series (their first since 1980) for themselves, their bonus money, future contacts, and—one presumes—diehard fans like me who would give almost anything to see these people (none of whom I know personally) succeed. As they struggle to reach the pinnacle of their profession, my mood will be affected greatly by the fortunes of my Eagles, who last earned a victory parade in 1960.

Of seemingly equal importance in my crazily jumbled entertainment world of sports, politics, and good versus evil is our watershed presidential election, the culmination of a campaign that seems to have lasted at least four years. My Democratic team seems to be suiting up a very promising young player who is taking on the team that has won the last two contests and ruled the executive branch of our sport for the last eight years, twenty-eight of the last forty. On the other side is a veteran opponent who I used to respect, but one who I have come to despise as if he was wearing the uniform of a Dallas Cowboy, New York Met, or a 1980s Boston Celtic.

All of this is must-watch TV, as were the Olympics and the political conventions. Win or lose (hey, my team wins once in awhile), I will either celebrate euphorically or vent my displeasure with gusto, but my guess is that the result will not really change me or the world all that much.

It is a sobering thought that my beautiful two-month-old baby is being affected by my mercurial moods as the TV is on almost constantly. I wonder what effect the screaming fanatics who are incapable of listening to reason—and those are just the candidates—have on him. What are the labels that he will start to identify with, and what type of bonds will we develop as a result?

There is hope in all this, as I picture his incomparably beautiful smile and dream of how he will contribute to a world that values intelligence, kindness, individualism, honesty, creativity, and a pure heart. I do all this as I monitor a Web site that features a political discussion board where there is one intelligent response for every five polarizing, insensitive rants. My daydream soldiers on as I listen to a sports radio talk show (at 3:30 am) that provides an outlet for Philly fans to vent after another crushing loss by my Eagles.

Go, teams!

The Fall of the Red Snow

November 2008

Prematurely or otherwise, I have decided to start writing my November column now, at 11:59 pm on October 26. Events between now and the posting of this column may make me wish to eat some of these words, but this is then, and now is the future. "*Huh?*" You ask for good reason.

Any day now, I expect to look out my window and see a bunch of men, women, children, and mailmen biting the dogs of my neighborhood. My eyes will perceive my beautifully manicured front lawn—or maybe said fictitious lawn will be covered with a coating of glorious, luxurious red snow.

For good measure, I will discover that my regimen of a Michael Phelps-like caloric consumption, four good hours of sleep a night, minimal exercise, and fifteen hours of television watching a day has put me in the greatest shape of my life. Brussels sprouts taste like prime rib; Sarah Palin is cerebral, classy, and open minded. Okay, that last one was even too strong for my fantasy sequence. But, bring on the champagne: my Philadelphia Phillies have w-w-wo ...

Well, they are so close to winning the first pro sports championship in these parts since 1983. Yes, twenty-five years and one hundred combined pro sports seasons of dogs biting men and ugly, slushy winters are about to come to an end. Just one more victory (and our superb young superstar lefty, Cole Hamels, is toeing the rubber in less than twenty-four hours) and the Phillies will have given the city with the collective inferiority complex—one that always plays second-fiddle to New York, Boston, D.C., and even Bayonne—another championship of our very own. We're just one win away, and with a three-games-to-one lead, we even have three chances to win it. We've got this one; I can feel it! That's why I'm sharing my thoughts with you now: if they let it get away, I'll be too depressed; if they hold on to it, I'll be too delirious.

Confidence is a very fleeting thing around here. The Phillies have shared their mostly meager existence with us fans since 1883, and have won exactly one world championship, in 1980. Ninety or so miles to our north, the Yankees have won twenty-six championships since 1923. Not sure what all this means, other than the fact that it takes a thick hide to have Philly pride. It takes tough skin to almost never win. But things are about to change, and I'm not sure exactly what that means for our teams, our city, my mood, my career, and my family's well-being.

Any baseball fans out there? Do you remember the infamous "Curse of the Bambino," a plague that devastated the Boston Red Sox from 1920 until 2004. As legend has it, a curse was placed on that franchise and their ultrarabid fans when their idiot owner sold the great Babe (Bambino) Ruth to the rival Yankees so he could finance his girlfriend's play. For the next eighty-four years, generations of Red Sox fans never enjoyed a championship while enduring the site of their cocky nemesis winning one championship after another—often eliminating the Red Sox in the process.

So what's my excuse for tasting this championship before it actually arrives in a city cursed even more than Boston was? Simple: my son, Benjamin (aka BJG), was born on July 24, 2008. Yes, he was born a few days too late to save my softball team from getting eliminated in the playoffs, but since his birth—and regardless of the amount of sleep I enjoyed the nights before—I have won all of my singles tennis matches. Okay, there have only been about six of them, but they *were* against evenly matched opponents. And now, Benny is inspiring my Phillies' ascent to the pinnacle of their sport. The Red Sox had the Curse of the Bambino; Philadelphia now has the **Blessing of the Ben-bino**. The forecast is for a lot of red snow in the years ahead, and dogs should not turn their backs on hungry mailmen.

At the Risk of Talking Politics

The 2008 election will very soon have an outcome, assuming no hanging chads or the like. I never intended to use this space to express my own political viewpoints, yet I knew that there would be plenty of opportunity to find humor in the day-to-day (or in this case, month-to-month) gaffes, missteps, strategies, and mindless coverage that the campaigns have engendered. It seems like five years ago that I wrote a somewhat satiric piece on all the candidates claiming to be "agents of change."

The finish line is now in sight; just eight days of punditry, prognostications, and political ads to slog our way through until we can actually cast our own votes. While there has been some humor to be mined from this campaign (thank you, Tina Fey, Jon Stewart, et al.), I am losing too much sleep and much of my good humor over the way almost everyone—from the candidates, their teams, the media, to friends and colleagues—has conducted themselves. There must be a better way to elect our leaders. Yes, there must be a much less protracted, much less expensive, and much more honorable and dignified process through which we conduct our elections.

Barring a late, late October or early November surprise, and if the majority of polls are correct, the candidate I am supporting—Barack Obama—will be the next president of the United States. If this happens, I don't know if I will experience more jubilation or relief. And then, in a couple months or so, I and many others will begin the process of evaluating whether he is a great, good, average, mediocre, or lousy commander-in-chief.

I have no way of knowing whether he will be a successful or even popular president, although I will tell you that even with his relative lack of experience, choosing him over John McCain has been an incredibly easy choice for me. In some ways, that is a disappointment to me, as I had always admired McCain.

One of the tragedies of 2008 is that precious little time on this campaign has been devoted to the actual issues, unless you count "lipstick on a pig/pit bull" as a substantive issue affecting millions of Americans when we are at war, in recession, and losing so much of our global prestige and respect. Call me a fool, but I thought a McCain-Obama match-up would offer such a discussion between respected rivals who articulate different political philosophies and prescriptions for getting America back on track. Will I ever learn my lesson?

So, come November 4 or 5, when I am experiencing great delight, relief, or depression over the results, I also hope to see an emphatic end to the following, in no particular order:

- Negative political ads
- The overall politics of personal destruction: smears, lies, innuendo, etc.
- An almost two-year election process with wall-to-wall coverage
- Massive donations to candidates that could be used instead to improve schools, build our infrastructure, feed and clothe the needy, etc.
- Political TV shows that have no sense of objectivity, dueling spin-doctors, and brainless journalism
- Campaigns (and media coverage) that have no respect for our intelligence
- Being told that I'm not patriotic or that I'm a communist/Marxist sympathizer because I disagree with a particular, extremely narrow viewpoint
- The utter lack of political courage by almost any candidate on the national scene
- E-mails from colleagues that are so full of hate, vitriol, and a lack of respect for others' opinions that I wonder if they even realize it
- Karl Rove, Steve Schmidt, and all of the architects of perhaps the most scattered, hate-filled, lowest common denominator general campaign I've ever witnessed
- Sarah Palin on the national political stage. It would be wonderful to see a qualified woman as a major party's nominee, or even as a running mate, if chosen for reasons other than pandering to the most cynical elements

> imaginable. I hope that her uninformed, narrow-minded, mean-spirited campaign will do nothing to either further her career or hurt the chances of eminently more qualified female candidates.

Having expressed my displeasure with our current process and many of its participants, I'm really not too jaded to daydream about shorter, less expensive, more respectful campaigns featuring candidates who are more honest and politically courageous than anyone I've seen in 2008. I also still have enough hope in *President Obama* to envision him as a thoughtful, dignified, articulate, uplifting presence in the White House who will do a solid job of steering us through these dangerous times and inspire others from all backgrounds to do even better for themselves and for others.

Conversely, I still have enough realism and pessimism to acknowledge that the Republicans may still hold onto the White House, yet the sun will still rise in the east the next day (even if virtually eclipsed by all of the dark, ominous clouds). But it is very early on the morning of October 27, and I need to try to get my four hours of sleep before starting my day—a day that will include a Phillies championship and a tomorrow filled with better times ahead for our country, blankets of red snow, and people who are so darn happy that they would never even think about biting a dog. Not even a pit bull.

MJG's note: In case you have been living in a parallel universe and the news didn't reach you, the Philadelphia Phillies—after a bizarre few days of rain delays, suspended games, and rainouts—won Game 5 by a 4-3 score to win their second ever World

Championship. Their win was rendered even more meaningful when the longtime "voice of the Phillies" (legendary, beloved Harry Kalas) passed away shortly into the 2009 season.

And in case you were wondering, my lawn is still blanketed by red snow and that is my excuse for not cutting it. In the Philly area alone, at least two hundred dogs of all breeds suffered mailman bites but seem to be doing better, and yes, the Phils are even looking like a favorite to repeat in 2009.

As for politics, my *team* won the 2008 election, and we'll see exactly what that will mean. Sarah Palin, you ask? Do I have to answer that? Ethics investigations, stream-of-consciousness stupidity, and a resignation from her gubernatorial post—all in the middle of her first term—have marked her last eight months or so. But this is America, and I'm not sure if we're collectively very forgiving or just very starstruck. With all that poor judgment, I fear that we have not heard the last of her, even on the national political stage. After all, regardless of whether it was spawned by fame or infamy, celebrity status is a big deal to us.

Best Stressed List

December 2008

Tons and tons of books, pamphlets, brochures, and DVDs have been produced with the purpose of informing us how stress can be so very harmful to our health. We all know that stress is to be avoided at all costs because it may lead to, in no particular order, many of the following conditions: gastrointestinal disorders, diabetes, heart disease, mental health issues, and a confused, ineffective immune system. This is all common knowledge.

There is also a readily available list of various common sense things that we can do to minimize the amount of stress in our lives in order to eat healthier, sleep better, and be in harmony with nature and our fellow men. Like almost everything else in life, the trick is not in finding this information; the trick is in putting belief behind it. If we learn *this* trick, then all we have to do is stay with the program for as long as we live.

All of the above has led me to my own conclusion: stress isn't all that bad after all. I don't have the scientific chops to refute medical evidence, and maybe I'm just being very pragmatic. I admit that I arrived at this theory after averaging about three hours of sleep a night over the past few weeks. My belly is crying more from being extended than distended, and my stack of unpaid bills would have to duck to not bump its head on your average cathedral ceiling. Junk food wrappers, McDonald's shake cups, and loose bagel seeds adorn my car's interior along with gas receipts and a few more unpaid bills that I forgot to bring inside the house.

So, what's my brand-new theory? It goes something like this: Yes, cutting down on stress may help me in countless ways, but it's not going to happen in my lifetime. The key to happiness, productivity, and peace of mind is in embracing and encouraging a stressful life. This will fuel my id (if not my ego), and it may help me squeeze out every ounce of creativity that I have to give.

Two notes on my theory. Others are welcome to subscribe to it, but I'm not yet at the point where I urge others to do so—stay tuned. The exact wording hasn't been approved yet by my legal department.

So why should we embrace and encourage stress in our lives? Have you ever heard of Vincent Van Gogh? He's one of the reasons. I'm sure you remember him—that post-Impressionist, pre-Expressionist Dutch artist who lopped off part of his own left ear. Van Gogh didn't start painting till he was twenty-seven, and he committed suicide at age thirty-seven. But in those final ten years, he produced roughly two thousand works, most of them the type of distinctive paintings that art connoisseurs all over the world would kill to own. Did I mention that Van Gogh spent most of those amazingly prolific years broke, weary, and mentally ill enough to chop off his left ear? Consider this: apparently, VVG had a neighbor named Tomas Van Dyk who ate all the right foods, slept eight hours a night, never drank, and lived to be ninety. Ever hear of Tomas Van Dyk? Didn't think so.

How's my theory doing? Need more data? Let's talk about the immortal Johannes Chrysostomus Wolfgangus Theophilus (Amadeus) Mozart, who some consider to be *the* classical musical genius of all time. And yes, his full name was practically as big as he was. In his scant thirty-five years on the planet, all Mozart did was compose a legendary six hundred classical works, some of which even a musical generalist like me would recognize. He must have led a very happy life, right? Think again. Mozart spent most of his days in poverty, married to a woman that his stern father disapproved of. Oh yeah, she gave birth to six of his children, only two of whom survived infancy.

Legend has it that Mozart showed up to many of his paid gigs drunk and quite disheveled. At one of his Vienna gigs, some nitwit who knew very little about him was quite unimpressed with his appearance. He asked Mozart, "Are *you* a composer?" To which Mozart, after *composing* himself, replied, "No, I'm a dais." (Insert groans here).

True story or not, Mozart was all of the following: broke, tired, sloppy, confused, and amazingly creative and prolific. He was stressed to the max but a certified genius who people will be celebrating for millennia to come.

The life lessons of Mozart and Van Gogh have given me just enough encouragement to expand upon and test my new theory. Why stress myself out over the best ways to lower my stress when I can enjoy the fruits of a no-worry, stress-filled life on my own terms? With the ghosts of Van Gogh and Mozart as my creative muses, I am determined to stop the charade of pretending to keep a balanced diet with the proper amounts of exercise and sleep.

Instead, I offer an easy-to-follow list of ways to increase your stress level and with it, your creative productivity. If creating like never before has the unintended consequence of reducing your stress again, so be it. Note: when I say "you", I mean "me," because I'm not yet ready to advocate this for all of you. So, enjoy this *best-stressed list (*yes, it spells out S-T-R-E-S-S), and feel free to jump in at your own peril.

Sleep Sporadically—Why worry yourself about getting your eight hours when you can be up eating, drinking, and doing whatever else makes you happy, productive, famous, and rich. And don't be concerned if most of your wealth and fame comes posthumously, as it did for Van Gogh and Mozart. To this end, I encourage myself to sleep at different times and different places (as a happily married man, I won't say "sleep with different people") as much as I can. I go to bed thinking of all the things I didn't do during the day with the express purpose of not sleeping too much or too well. If this becomes hard to do, I count unpaid bills as if they were sheep. I always try to remember that a lack of sleep will make me irritable, agitated, and edgy. It is this edginess that I endeavor to bring to my life, as well as to my art.

Try Triglycerides—This one should be a snap. Don't stress too much over your lipid profile; just boost your LDL with a semilethal combo of some of the best stuff that life has to ingest: fats, alcohol, and carbohydrates. The beauty of this is that doing so will help you sleep sporadically and you can take this approach to the next level by engaging in the ingestion of triglycerides during normal sleeping hours. While enjoying your fat sandwich over a beer or two, write a page or two of deathless prose, paint a nude model, or compose a sonata.

Resist Routine—Routine will only rid you of your natural inclinations to stay up late, eat all sorts of good crap, and generally enjoy life. My one word of advice is that you shouldn't resist routine too religiously, or that may box you into a whole new routine. So in other words, when you feel like it, go against the grain. And if that approach becomes too ingrained, try something else. Hey, whatever keeps you up at night.

Enough Exercise—Why go to the trouble of skimping on sleep and not following a sensible diet if you're going to piss it all away by exercising too much? Makes no sense to me. So be moderate in your exercise with the following exception: If you have not exercised much recently, you should do so intensively a couple days in a row, making sure to overexert those same areas. The likely result? Injury, less sleep, and more late-night binging.

Skip Sex—Okay, sex is a great form of exercise and a great way to express your love and lust with the partner of your choice. Or so I've heard. (I am the undersexed father of a beautiful, four-month-old baby.) What am I advocating? Skip sex, like Muhammad Ali used to do before heavyweight title fights. Stay just a little angry, agitated, and nonmellow. In the long run, you may even be happier as a result.

Start Smoking—Despite the abundance of research, technology, and support groups, a very small percentage of smokers are able to successfully kick their habits. So don't kick the habit; start a new habit. Just smoke at random and don't make it too big a part of your routine. Do it at different times but don't smoke enough to curb your appetite and enthusiasm for fats and sweets. Don't light up after sex; light up *instead* of sex and do it as a substitute for more acceptable forms of exercise.

Well, there you have it. My best stressed list theory is still in its infancy and I hope to have some updates for you over time. If you wish to share your own stories—and you should have plenty of free time that was once devoted to sleep—go ahead. Unlike Van Gogh, I'm all ears.

2009

9 for 2009?

January 2009

Almost halfway between Christmas and New Year's, I am glancing at the contents that filled this space exactly one year ago. I shudder to look at my "Resolutionary Ideas" column of last year. It is like facing a pile of unpaid bills or a solar eclipse directly with my naked eyes. Forging on, I find that I haven't done so well on my 2008 scorecard, although I still have three and a half days to lose the twenty-one pounds needed to achieve my goal of losing fifteen pounds. In case you were wondering, I am not *the biggest loser.*

Is it any wonder that I don't make resolutions every year? Last week, I thought that I would try for "9 for 2009." It has an obvious ring to it, and it is not as cliché as a top ten list. The number "9" also suggests, in my mind anyway, the improbable World Series title of 2008 won by my Philadelphia Phillies—9 players pulling together over 9 innings to win the first major pro sports title in Philly in about 9 zillion years. Resolution, revolution ... number 9, number 9, number 9 ... Beatles-inspired puns aside, I will forego the nine resolution strategy, if not the pun.

I'm just not resolute enough to make resolutions. Oh, almost everyone I've met in life would describe me as an honest, well-meaning guy. It's just that I tend to keep my well-intentioned resolutions as well as politicians keep their mostly self-serving promises; I don't, yet I leave enough wiggle room to weasel a good excuse or two. In the world of resolutions—those time-honored promises to self—I play the roles of both the politician and his hapless constituent. I overpromise *and* I deliver less. Sadly, after four-plus decades on this planet, it has gotten very easy to break my promises to myself. One other sobering discovery: it has gotten almost as easy to forgive myself for doing so ...

Nearing the end of 2008, I am typing away in a euphemism called my home office, where barbells, CDs, VHS tapes, and DVDs vie for space with thousands of business cards, brochures, flashing lights, keepsakes of every imaginable category and value, papers, office supplies, checkbooks, and real books—including my own unsold masterpieces. I'm probably making my workspace sound more appealing than it really is—you'd have to be here to appreciate just how quickly I can junk up a room. If you need a corroborating expert witness, just ask my wife Ruby.

Just outside my basement office/bunker, is my once highly prized ping-pong table. The same surface that I used to keep in great shape (okay, the dampness was slowly warping it, but it was still a terrific playing surface) for my infrequent death matches with the few challengers each year who would enter my lair, is now folded in half.

The unfolded half now contains a frightening morass of unpaid bills, notices, letters, magazines, and junk mail. This cornucopia of crapola is covered with an old blanket. Pandora's blanket? I lift it occasionally, afraid to face the scorecard of my financial life. Every night, the blanket covers my record-keeping nightmare. I don't gently tuck in the contents; I am assured that they will sleep well, even if I won't.

Upstairs, my eleven-year-old niece, from New York by way of China, is sleeping soundly on the living room sofa. How do I know? The TV is off. "Cathy" is a very bright if somewhat shy and stubborn kid who has seemed to master the English language after only a year and a half in the United States. Other than Cartoon Network and Alexander, my indefatigable, sleep-resistant, almost four-year-old nephew, I have been the main source of her entertainment. We played three games of chess yesterday—nearly every move would make Bobby Fischer (wherever he is) spit in disgust—capped by a near-marathon Monopoly game. I am pleased to have won two out of three chess games and I skunked her in the Parker Brothers classic, somehow ending up with thirteen hotels, after keeping her alive a couple times with mercy deals. Cathy will be here for another six days; I'm sure she will exact her revenge, or at least try repeatedly to do so.

In the kitchen, my mother-in-law is active and helpful as always, unintentionally putting all of us to shame. Up a half level, Ruby's sister Linda, aka Alex's mom, seems to be sleeping, and Ruby (when I checked on her after the third paragraph) was nursing *BJG,* our perfect five-month-old, who seems to be fighting the second cold of his existence. Correction: he's nearly perfect.

If all goes well, I will sneak out of the house sometime between 1 and 4:00 pm to catch most of *NFL Sunday* with a pal from high school days. By the time our Eagles square off with the Cowboys at 4:15 pm, we will know if they are fighting for a playoff spot—and a theoretical shot at their first ever Super Bowl win—or merely playing the role of spoilers, ending the loathsome Cowboys' own shot at making the playoffs. Either way, it's "must-see TV", and I have some mixed feelings as to whether similar games will become *must-see TV* over the years for BJG. I have had the challenge of holding my Benny through a couple of Eagles games, trying to pat him reassuringly, or giving him *airplane* rides with a steady hand, while my team is making me apoplectic.

For all concerned, it is imperative that I leave the house this time for reasons both unselfish (preserving Benny's health and sanity) and selfish. No doubt, Cathy will be watching cartoons, or Alex will be watching the same talking cars DVD for the sixteenth time on the one good TV, relegating me to an uncomfortable chair in my office bunker squinting at a smallish TV with poor resolution.

Speaking of poor resolutions, if I stayed committed to nine resolutions for 2009, they may look something like this (I am now writing them for the first time, and in strictly off-the-top-of-the-head order):

1. Be a great family member in all respects—son, brother, son-in-law, brother-in-law, uncle, and of course, husband and father.

2. Either work harder at my business or develop my writing business. Either way, make more money (earned or otherwise, if ethical) in 2009 and create something resembling a game plan for 2010 and beyond.

3. Okay, shed some pounds and approximate the shape I'd like to be in.

4. Find a solution to the ongoing drama of trying to tolerate some of my mother-in-law's cooking. In brief, she is a good cook and a great lady, but some of her black bean meets pepper spray dishes are not only inedible for me, but I can't even breathe

within a two-mile radius of such cuisine without getting nauseated. No palatable solutions have been found so far, as it's doubtful that any of these events will happen next year: a) she'll stop cooking these childhood favorites of hers; b) I'll suddenly be able to coexist with this noxious aroma; c) we'll move into a gigantic mansion; or d) a strong enough candle will be invented that will allow such peaceful olfactory coexistence without harming the ozone layer.

5. Publish my children's book, revive my alter ego, *So So Gai*, and become a paid columnist.

6. Break some of my addiction to watching TV—especially sports.

7. Read more.

8. Read more with my son and write some books with him—and countless other kids and parents—in mind.

9. Increase my hours of community service, not the court-ordered kind.

Admittedly, the above list is kind of impressive and not too imposing, yet I will treat it as what it is—a column filler. I've learned my oft-repeated lesson; I'm not going to make any resolutions. It's imperative that I don't look back at this column one year from now and feel like a sleazy, corrupt politician *and* a disillusioned citizen. No, I am not going to set up a cycle of disappointment (or worse) made inevitable by my mercurial psyche and irresolute nature.

Make that, "*may* not."

Flushing Away

February 2009

Out with the Old, and in with the Ox?

The Chinese New Year—"out with the (year of the) rat, and in with the ox"—started in a promising enough fashion. Ruby, her Mom, and our six-month-old, Baby Ben, left the house for our weekend trip to Flushing (part of Queens, New York City—*that* Flushing) in almost record time—only two hours behind schedule. Cruising through the relatively sparse traffic, we made it to Ruby's sister's at a reasonable hour, and were greeted by our almost twelve-year-old niece, and later joined by both of Ruby's sisters, her brother-in-law, and our almost four-year-old nephew. Yes, it was almost time to greet the Year of the Ox, and it was also Ruby's sister's birthday—almost.

The nine of us celebrated in keeping with our joint family tradition—eating enough quality Chinese food for a village of one hundred. I exaggerate; Baby Ben's not eating solid foods yet so we collectively ingested only enough food for a hamlet of ninety. One of the dishes included long, long noodles eaten to wish Tan Jie a long, healthy life, it being the evening before her birthday. I forget all of the foods that I personally consumed and, except for most of the contents of a box of tea (projected almost horizontally out of the gullet of our dear nephew, Alexander, who was fighting a cold—nobody was hurt or badly splattered), the evening ended without much drama. Indeed, there was enough love and good spirit in the room to welcome any birthday lady or friendly ox.

When in Flushing, Do as The ...

Saturday morning arrived with more food, as Birthday Girl picked up a large number of foodstuffs that I have come to know (and usually love) as *baozi*. Ruby and I had first crack, as the rest of the family was out and about. This calls for a word or two about Chinese cuisine from this American with a substantial, if sometimes uncultured, appetite. Flushing has one of the largest Chinatown areas in the U.S. and as such, all types of restaurants, produce markets, and mostly delicious takeout food is within an easy walk from her sister's apartment. A baozi (you're on your own with the correct pronunciation) is a steamed bun of sorts, usually filled with meat or maybe pork, and sometimes vegetables as well.

A few more notes about baozi:

1. The best baozi seems to be the pork-filled one. Having grown up keeping kosher, I only eat those filled from pigs that say "moo" and chew their own cud. I always ask first.
2. My assiduous research assistant informs me that the literal translation of baozi is "(baozi) that dogs ignore." Would my source lie?
3. This particular batch of baozi may have been the tastiest I have ever wolfed down,

including a famous batch of soup baozi I thoroughly enjoyed in Shanghai.

Filled with the tasty food that dogs are said to ignore, Ruby and I ventured into the extreme cold and wind to walk the few blocks to the heart of Chinatown on Main Street. Baby Ben, ever the trooper, uttered nary a complaint nor cry during our whole two-hour walk, and indeed, he was bundled up as if he were discarded for a week on the steppes of Mongolia. Any fans of *A Christmas Story* out there? Think kid brother Randy on his first day of school, but zipped up in a stroller.

It seemed like I spent almost three of those two hours inside an indoor/outdoor produce market with my stroller backed up against the grapefruit display while Ruby zipped around the store. After several futile attempts, she finally found a line where there was a cashier on duty. While waiting for Ruby to check out, there must have been at least one hundred people entering and about eighty exiting the medium-sized market. Oddly and luckily enough, nobody was really in the market for grapefruits. Benny slept through it all and uttered not a word—Mandarin or otherwise.

Back home, about eight more courses of food were prepared, including a beautiful cake Ruby made for Birthday Girl. Good thing, as the nine of us had to be starving from our *skimpy* Friday night repast. Now we were trying to eat at a quickened pace, as I was going to accompany my niece to a new Broadway show, titled *Soul of Shaolin*. A little music, a little violence, and maybe even another snack. You know, in these situations, I kind of just roll with the punches, shoveling down any food that is somewhat familiar. When in Flushing ...

If any of you have seen *Soul of Shaolin,* please let me know if it lived up to its hype. We almost made it there. When exiting the apartment building, Ruby's brother-in-law was stopped by a policeman who said that we would have to remain inside while a police investigation was underway in the building. We checked back with the cop a couple more times in the next half hour, but to no avail; the investigation—something suspicious was happening above our basement apartment—would continue until about noon the next day. Oh, if any of you know what happened on Chinese New Year's weekend in a nondescript, four-story Flushing apartment building across from a little park near Main Street, please let us know.

But as I reflect upon it now, it seems to make sense in keeping with the theme of the weekend. There must have been a rat or two upstairs and the cop was being stubborn as an ox. Appropriate enough for the occasion. We also could not leave the building even to see a show in Manhattan about Chinese martial arts. "Martial law at its finest," I thought.

Sequestered inside for the evening, we did what any other family would do. Eat more cake, play with the kids, and watch Benny's multitalented uncle give my shaggy little boy his third haircut. Success on all counts, making for a little sleep ...

... which lasted for minutes until the revenge of the rat—or was it the cake, the baozi, or an Asian-American flu? Whatever it was (and I still say those were the best baozi I've ever had) kept me up at least ten times to visit their one and only bathroom. I will spare you a lot of messy details, but will tell you the obvious: I spent the night doing a whole lot of, um, flushing.

It's a terrible thing to be awake in the middle of the night, and without the ability to access a computer, a television, or a place to read without waking up family members with more regular bowels. The freshly shorn Baby Ben was among those able to sleep through the night quite well and I spent the first hours of Sunday praying that I could do anything—even change a diaper—other than dumping and flushing.

Feed a Cold, and … Then What?

As morning came, I didn't try to remember that old adage "starve a cold and feed a fever." Something like that, right? I usually can't remember which to starve and which to feed (if I know what I'm fighting to begin with), so I tend to feed a fever, stuff a cold, and gorge myself when flu-ridden. Only this Flushing Flu was serious stuff, and I would end up eating nothing more substantial than plain crackers and Jell-O for the first two days of the Year of the Ox. If there's poetic justice in not being able to eat like an ox at the beginning of that animal's year, then it's lost on me. Poetic or not, I do figure that there are lessons to be learned from my almost healthy New Year's weekend in Flushing, including:

- If your only child was born in the Year of the Rat, don't be so quick to bid it good-bye and move on to the next animal.
- Always pack that bottle of your favorite regulating liquid beverage, especially if you may be staying in a building with no medicine labels you understand, and you may be quarantined for a police investigation.
- I still have to find out where my sister-in-law got those amazing baozi. They were worth the drive to Flushing—almost!

- After spending the weekend flushing in Flushing, I decree that we will spend next year in beautiful Intercourse, Pennsylvania. Martial law optional.

Dentally Challenged

March 2009

Coming to terms with our personal feelings toward dentistry is a part of all our lives, be they full or like mine. Just last week, I had the pleasure of going to my dentist for a permanent crown and a long-term filling. I was a little excited about the procedure; as inevitabilities go, it ranked ahead of both death and taxes, if just on a par with getting fatter and growing balder. But over the years, I have realized that the key to any good dental visit is staying calm. As delighted as I once may have been to have one of my teeth elevated to crown status, I am also becoming somewhat of a veteran of such transactions. So I felt an air of reassurance about me as I crossed the threshold into Dr. Chew's office. And, no, I am not quite shameless enough to invent that name.

Following the office protocol, I signed in with one of the *Chew-ettes*, who gave me a greeting that was nice enough for the occasion, if I ignore the fact that she identified me as *Matthew*—a given name that suggests to me that I did something wrong. But not to worry. My first visit to that office the previous week had been uneventful enough, a huge compliment that any self-respecting practice of this profession would gladly accept. And the compliment was warranted. The dental assistant, while no Heidi Klum, exhibited the qualities that the older, wiser me have come to appreciate. She was soft-spoken yet communicated clearly about each step that was taking place. She even laughed at a couple of my wisecracks—always a sign of intelligence and nobility. The yellow patient's chair was almost comfy, and there was a nice TV perched at just the right angle, so I could watch Dr. Phil before bending down to spit saliva and blood into the side-of-the-chair basin. Even Dr. Peck—partner of the mysterious Dr. Chew, whom I have never seen—reeked of competence and even-handedness, good traits for any dentist.

As I waited for my esteemed tooth whisperer to escort me from the waiting room to the chair of honor, I walked over to the two large fish tanks in the back of the room. My keen and perceptive eyes beheld a bunch of silver and orange fish swimming around the rectangles. I zeroed in on one of the little Nemos, the tunnel vision producing just the right measure of whimsy and serenity that I needed. Transfixed as I was by the little orange guy, I turned around just in time to see what I suspected was the most beautiful dental patient ever sighted in a South Jersey practice—other than my wife, of course. When she turned around, her front view confirmed my suspicions. I took a seat as far away from Nemo as I could and felt some guilty pleasure as the hot brunette took a seat next to me. Exactly five seconds later, my good fortune was immediately shattered by the loudest female voice I have ever heard this side of a good prison movie.

"Matthew, come on back, Matthew ... how you doing today?" thundered the Roseanne Barr sound-alike. After giving me three nanoseconds to respond to her largely rhetorical question, she vocally barged ahead, "Oh, you're doing that well, huh? Well, follow me." Preternaturally, her voice just kept getting louder and faster. Louder and faster it rambled as I followed my executioner to the dreaded yellow chair.

Turning my gaze to the waiting room, I swear that I saw Nemo and Dory trying to swim out of the tank. I then caught the eye of my dental dream girl, who seemed to be laughing—but in a most appealing way—at my misery. The practical joke would soon be over, wouldn't it? Roseanne Barr and Frieda Pinto would soon be changing places, and all would be well in dental-land, right? Instinctively, I then did what any self-respecting Jew would never admit to doing in this situation. I *prayed on it*.

"So, you're having a cap replaced, and another filling, do you remember what teeth they were, I think it was #15 and #56-B, and ... "

Prayer denied, I thought, as my mind conjured up some ghosts of dental visits past ...

... There used to be a time in my life when going to the dentist was so simple. My parents would drive my older brothers, Dan and Josh, and me in the family clunker to see Dr. Mortimer Beller for our annual checkups. Dr. Beller and his wife were fellow synagogue members and friends of the family, a quite exclusive club by the way. My memories of those visits are limited, but pleasant. We would go to Mort's office and wait our turns to see him. Dr. Beller, a large and largely round gregarious man, would greet us with a joke or some small talk before getting down to business. The highlight of each visit was seeing Mort bounce a Dixie Cup off his bicep and catch it—a trick we all tried to perfect home with Mom's kooky assortment of sentimental plastic and glass tumblers. Before we left the office, we would be congratulated on having no cavities and encouraged to brush most of our teeth a couple times a day with fluoride toothpaste. That's what I remember; I would ask Dan if that is totally accurate, but this is a recollection and not a research project.

Our home dental care program was also delightfully simple. We would go into our 1962-designed bathroom where the three of us would each use toothbrushes of our favorite colors, along with an almost matching toothpaste cup that would find its way to the dishwasher twice a year, whether it needed cleansing or not. We three brothers would apply some generic brand toothpaste—or a name brand, on the rare occasions when Mom had enough coupons to buy the upscale stuff—and brush away about twice a day, whether our teeth needed the attention or not. There was also a mysterious, and never used, bottle of mouthwash that was visible and visibly dirty under the powder blue sink, and alas, flossing had not worked its way into our collective consciousness yet.

When I was about ten years old, the Goldberg kids did alter their tooth brushing routine to take advantage of the latest technology. Mom came home one day with an electric toothbrush set that Dad mounted on the bathroom wall, covering up a sailboat or two on our hideous wallpaper. I recall that we used the set for about two weeks before the novelty and some of our enamel wore off. This technological wonder was the oral hygienic cousin of electric football; the power came on, the decibel level tripled, and then nothing much happened. Still, that experiment was honored in typical Goldberg style. When my parents sold our childhood home about thirty-three years later, the electric toothbrush case was still mounted to what was left of the nautical wallpaper.

Little did I appreciate that I was actually living in dental heaven. Heaven was a time and a place where

I could eat whatever I wanted in massive quantities and never need a single filling or crown. How could I possibly imagine that I would one day stop inhaling copious amounts of candy and chocolate milk, resulting in loss of hair, gain of belly, and decay of tooth? It sucks being healthy and knowledgeable.

By the time I arrived in college, at least five years had passed since my last dental checkup. Apparently, Dr. Beller had moved out of the area, and nobody else in our intimate circle of family friends was proficient at scraping tartar off of our molars. College was a time to expand my mind by cutting class, watching old TV shows on twelve-inch black-and-white sets, sampling once-foreign *pharmaceuticals*, and discussing anything and everything to make sense of the world. While I'm not sure what I remember about these discussions (other than my college buddies talking about how hot the dental hygienists were), I did, by necessity, stumble upon an important theory of frugal dental care.

After unceremoniously dropping my toothbrush in the toilet bowl, I decided that my $1.50 would be better spent on beer than a replacement set of bristles. Hey, money was tight, and living alone called for executive decisions of all kinds. So, I spent at least one semester using my right index finger as my personal toothbrush. Although this behavior may have been evidence of a large cavity developing in my brain, my teeth never felt better. There's a lesson in there somewhere, kids.

As I recall, it wasn't until a few years after my miraculous college graduation that I went to a dentist other than Dr. Beller. Several things still stand out about that visit:

- The dental hygienist (first I had ever seen) was smoking hot.

- After years of throwing caution to the wind and brushing with an actual toothbrush, I had my first cavities ever.
- The whole process—other than drooling over the hygienist—was a pain in my burgeoning posterior. And nobody even asked me about my family or bounced cups to entertain me.
- Did I mention the hygienist? My college buddies weren't total idiots after all.

As more years passed, I became increasingly more frightened by the dentist and more enamored of the hygienist, who apparently had their union change their name to dental assistants about the time that stewardesses became flight attendants. But invariably, even as my medical insurance had me switching dental practices more often than I replaced toothbrushes, I still found all members of that union incredibly attractive. Well, except for one or two, but maybe they were scabs.

Now before you convict me for being just another shallow male who is guilty of objectifying an entire profession, do consider this. As I have grown longer in the tooth, I have also matured slightly. My candy ingestion has not ceased, but it has lessened. I don't watch as many cartoons and sitcoms as I used to, and I tend to appreciate other attributes from women besides the obvious ones.

But lines need to be drawn somewhere. If the woman who pokes her latex gloved hand in my mouth is not the sweetest eye candy, so be it. I can handle that, but I can't handle that glove smelling like a cigar shop. And, I do ask that the lady who will be an accessory to putting me through some of the most painful moments in the human experience have better manners than your garden-variety neighborhood wombat. Since one of my, um, tooth tormentresses flunked out on those two litmus tests, I stopped going to that office and dentists altogether for another seven years. And to this day, every time, I see an unattractive thirtyish woman smoking a cigarette outside a Wawa, I picture Ms. Wombat shoving her smoky, fisted glove into my mouth.

With all this time between visits, not to mention all the time prior to producing a rant about my obvious dental retardation, my mind would pause to consider the following question that has haunted mankind since the first bar mitzvah boy was forced to wear braces. How come men will put themselves through all kinds of pain if there is a gorgeous dental *hy-sistant* nearby? Are we just trying to display our cool, on the snowball's chance that Ms. Dental Babe will be impressed and show up naked to our poker games? Is the combination of Novocain and cleavage enough to overpower an electric drill spinning inside a desperate man's mouth? I'm still haunted ...

... My dental background being what it was, I snapped out of my recollections long enough to somewhat willingly open up my pie hatch. Ms. Foghorn commanded me to spit out my gum, and informed half of the residents of South Jersey that there was some mouthwash on the basin that I could use to rinse and spit. Ignoring the preferred bull's-eye on top of her neck, I took dead aim for the little white basin. Asking for a tissue, my captor regaled me about how she had the ingenuity to Velcro the box of tissues to the table that supported the television. I quickly nodded to acknowledge her resourcefulness and then plaintively looked up at the television for any relief in sight. As Mr. Ed is my witness, the blasted tube was on the blink.

Although internally jonesing for something soothing like Dr. Phil, even Jerry Springer, in an ironic sense I had gotten my wish. I had returned to a simpler time and place, where the dental office had no TV sets or beautiful assistants.

After two doses of Novocain, I would somehow endure what felt like fifty-five hours of drilling by Dr. Peck, the drill rendered virtually inaudible by Roseanne's endless babbling. In fact, when the tooth shatterer wasn't prattling on about something, she was uproariously laughing into what was left of my left eardrum. I was starting to feel sorry for Dr. Peck, who had to work with this *farce of nature* on an ongoing basis. However, I immediately stopped feeling sorry for this man when I considered the following:

- He was making a lot of dough to make me feel like warmed-up excrement.
- He had this terrible habit of using my anesthetized mouth as a storage area for his implements, to say nothing of his penchant for drilling straight into my gums.
- He would be able to eat whatever he wanted, whenever he wanted; I was advised to wait at least an hour before challenging my teeth with some oatmeal.

My unforgiving nature intact, I climbed out of the padded, mechanical chair and followed the object of my now recurring dental nightmares to the receptionist's desk. It was time for the all-important remittance of the copay. Asked to make an appointment for the following week to fill the other wisdom tooth, I declined their generous offer. In my heart, I knew that nothing too catastrophic could go wrong if I waited another seven years or so for my next dental visit.

On my drive home, I daydreamed about a new dental practice that would feature a working TV, a nonsmoking, velvet-voiced babe of a hy-sistant, and a dentist with more refined drillmanship. I decided that Nemo, Dory, and patients with supermodel looks were a luxury that I could not count on—even in my daydreams.

Killing time until I could eat again, I cleverly bought a jar of matzo ball soup. Soft, soothing—what's not to like? When I returned home to an empty house, I instantly put my feet up on the recliner, zapped on my working TV, and realized that while the Novocain was not strong enough to dull the pain of the drill or the voice of the she-devil, it would make the right side of my mouth feel numb for about six more hours. With eating not an option, I settled for my second favorite pastime—sleep.

In time, I would wake up with a combination headache/toothache, the memory of which would serve as a cautionary tale of sorts on the evils of visiting the modern dental office. But before this reality check would take hold, I was back in the land of the gregarious dentist and the never- ending, never-fattening cartons of chocolate milk. A heavily stained sailboat carrying a green, electric toothbrush cruised with me into my childhood kitchen. Grabbing a glass from the dishwasher—one with the likeness of Archie and Jughead on it that my Mom had gotten for free—I paused before opening the refrigerator door.

Unrolling my shirtsleeves, I turned Jughead upside down and directed him toward my finely toned little bicep. Missing its target, the complementary glass hit the linoleum and shattered as if it were a ritualistic prop at a Jewish wedding. "No problem, we have plenty more glasses," I was thinking, as Dan and Josh nodded their heads almost approvingly.

Reaching for a green plastic tumbler, I heard the sweet, familiar voice of my Mom of blessed memory. “Matthew,” she cried out, “you didn’t break that Jughead glass, did you? You know that was my favorite.”

A Tale of Two Spring Trainings

April 2009

Each year in the dead of winter, we baseball fans celebrate that hopeful day in mid-February when one of the most beautiful five-word phrases in the English language is proclaimed—"Pitchers and catchers report (to spring training) today." As a harbinger of warm weather, it's much more pleasing than that other, hackneyed five-word phrase—"Groundhog Day, Groundhog Day, Groundhog … "

By the time March rolls around, the other Major League Baseball position players join the pitchers and catchers at spring training. They work out in various small towns in balmy Florida or sunny Arizona to prepare for the long season ahead. Optimism generally reigns in these locales and many fans fly south to these warm spots to also rejuvenate their own bodies and spirits.

This year, my Philadelphia Phillies are about to wrap up their spring training in the beautiful, quaint town of Clearwater, Florida. They play in a gorgeous stadium complex, where the infields are immaculate, and the grass is the shade of green that makes even the most hard-hearted cynics get a little tingly. Proving that this is no *Groundhog Day* scenario, the Phillies will do something that they haven't had to do but one other time in their mostly dismal 126-year history: attempt to defend their title of World Champions. The notoriously tough Philly fans have renewed their love affair with the Phils, an affair that should last till at least April 15 or so.

In the humdrum, nonquaint suburb of Cherry Hill, New Jersey, my Mkor Shalom synagogue softball team (no nickname, but we're open to suggestions) renewed practice on the fields provided by the local schools. Infields are bumpy and as brown as the Kansas prairies. Any fans that show up are there by accident, or because they are taking a respite while their dogs do their business by the side of the fence.

Major League Baseball (MLB) has been around since 1876, and now boasts of thirty teams, divided somewhat evenly—sixteen in the National League, and fourteen in the American League. During spring training, all of the teams head for beautiful little spots like Clearwater. Sixteen teams play in the Florida Grapefruit League, and fourteen play in the Arizona Cactus League. These (mostly) world-class athletes, the best the sport has to offer, fine-tune their bodies in gorgeous weather for the grueling, 162-game regular season that opens in April.

The Jewish Athletic Group (JAG) softball league—which I have rightfully nicknamed the Oxymoron League—is starting its twelfth year of somewhat competitive play. Since 8:45 am can be quite frigid in early March in Cherry Hill, we attempt to hold our version of spring training in the southern part of Cherry Hill, where on the

right day the temperature may be .005 degrees warmer than in the northern reaches of town.

The Oxymoron league is divided into a more competitive "A" division (where I still hang) and a "B" division. Last year, five teams played in "A" and nine played in "B." This year, the powers-that-be kept the 5 A-teams intact, added another team, and now place five teams in B, and five in C. Perhaps we are the best players that our respective synagogues have to offer, and that's a scary thought. On those rare March Sundays where it isn't raining or snowing, we drag our overweight, rigid selves around the *brownswards* of Cherry Hill, pretending to lose two pounds each time we round the bases.

Those lucky enough to make a MLB roster are guaranteed a minimum annual salary of about $400,000. The average salary is just south of three million dollars. Of course, that does not include a slew of other perks such as per diem meal allowances, endorsement deals, and five-star hotels.

All Oxymoron League players pay for the privilege of playing Sunday softball, the fee to be set by the *sponsoring* synagogues. This year, the men of Mkor paid $115 for the privilege of playing; those who registered after March 1 paid an additional $25. Of course, this doesn't count a slew of other expenses such as synagogue dues (a minimum of $2,000 plus other fund drives), softball equipment, and other necessities such as water bottles, Advil, and oxygen tanks.

My Phillies are led by their manager, the enigmatic but lovable (he's considered to be lovable, now that the team has won a World Series for its long-suffering fans) Charlie Manuel. Charlie is sixty-five years old and looks eighty-five, speaks in a southern drawl, and tends to commit the sort of malapropisms that belie how much he truly knows about baseball. But good ol' *Chollie* is what is known as a "player's manager"; indeed, his players seem to love his folksy, avuncular style and they play their butts off for him.

My Mkor (Muskrats?) are led by two co-captains, who got their lofty positions mostly because nobody else wanted them. They are about forty-five and fifty years old, respectively, and look about forty-five and fifty for that matter. The younger one of the two seems to now come to the field reluctantly, as he is now more into playing street hockey (not recognized as a sport by JAG). The other captain is a heart-and-soul player, who, like yours truly, seems to always be playing through an injury or three. Both play hard and well—for this level of play—and the rest of us also play as hard as we can, as we realize that this is most likely our last bastion of competitive play.

The Phillies will leave Clearwater with the twenty-five players that will start the regular season in Philadelphia. It is an honor to make the twenty-five-man roster, and, of course, it is financially rewarding as well. A few players will get cut during the final week and have to settle for playing for one of the team's minor league clubs at a lower salary. When the Phils play at beautiful Citizens Bank Park, they typically play in front of a near-sellout crowd of 43,500 diehard fans.

My Mkor A-team came into this season with the goal of having fourteen or fifteen guys on our roster. As of this writing, with less than a week to go before the start of the season, we have exactly eleven. We lost four players from last year's team, and it was somehow determined that three or four new guys did not have what it takes to play for our juggernaut, which happened to finish fifth in our five-team division last year. In all fairness, we did make the finals the previous four years, but our reputation for taking things too seriously has apparently discouraged others from playing with us. So these poor rejected accountants, doctors, and lawyers will settle for playing in the B division. A typical regular season attendance for a JAG doubleheader (B or A) is roughly 4.5 somewhat interested family members.

The amazing, ageless Jamie Moyer, still one of the Phillies' better pitchers, is MLB's oldest player at forty-six years old. The average Phillies player is about twenty-nine years old. Jamie, highly respected by both his teammates and his fans, is called *Grandpa* by some of the younger players, a term of endearment—sort of.

Jamie Moyer would be one of our youngest players on a roster that probably averages about forty-eight years old. Indeed, he would be our youngest pitcher—our staff led by yours truly. This is a sobering thought. Two years ago, we did have a player who could have called me "Grandpa." I wouldn't take kindly to that term, of course, and would consider kicking his butt, but for two reasons: 1) he was only seventeen years old, and 2) he weighed about three hundred pounds. His dad, a

few years my senior, is our second pitcher and once had to sit out a doubleheader after his humongous son (accidentally?) nailed him in the thigh with a batting practice line drive. Dad's a good guy and allegedly pays his son's tuition to college, where he plays on his football team's offensive line.

Most MLB pitchers throw fastballs at speeds greater than ninety-two or so miles per hour, and even their "off-speed" pitches that slide and dive away from batters travel at about eighty.

On my best day as a high school baseball pitcher, I probably threw my fastball at around seventy-three. Now we play with bigger balls (you know what I mean), which travel at maybe ten mph thrown at an arc between six and twelve feet at its apex. As if we needed a reminder that our best days are in the rear view mirror of life, the Oxymoron League replaced the traditional white balls with these ugly, nearly phosphorescent green-yellow ones.

It has been evident for quite some time that I will never fulfill one of my childhood dreams—that of being a major league baseball player. But even now, a good fifteen to twenty years past my prime (which wasn't that prime to begin with), I get a certain rush from being out there with the guys, diving all over and getting my uniform dirty, chattering on the field and in the dugout (okay, it's a tiny bench in the grass-dirt), and even arguing occasionally with the umpires. And yes, I have to pay for the privilege of playing, but I still get bummed out when games, or even practices, are rained out. I still want every ball to be hit to me in the field, and I still get excited when I can swing a bat to knock in a run or two for my team. I still get that extra hop in my step as Sunday morning approaches.

Indeed, every spring, whether my balls are getting bigger or simply softer, my dream in some small measure is still alive.

MJG's note: For those dying to know, my team ended up with an 11-9 regular season, bouncing back from a dispiriting 0-5 start to achieve some level of competence. We added a twelfth player and shockingly never had to forfeit a game for lack of bodies. Surprisingly, nobody quit midseason or suffered a season-ending injury. My back went out after the first week, but after a lot of chiropractic appointments, returned to the field—at whatever strength—two weeks later. Incredibly, we had no rainouts or snowouts for the first season in memory, yet we always seemed to be playing on a wet, muddy field.

Our record was good enough for third place, and we were *good* enough to be swept in two reasonably close games by the second place team. Our conquerors won the championship three weeks later, after sitting out the July 4 weekend and the following Sunday as well, out of respect for the annual JAG picnic.

The kosher dogs and burgers at the JAG picnic were pretty good, thanks mostly to our league commissioner, known simply as Turtle. So why does a fifty-plus-year-old (Jewish) man and softball junkie call himself "Turtle," and what can I tell you about this character?

Now, *that's* a future column.

Scenes from an Incompetent Life

May 2009

In just a few hours, at the Coffee Works Café in Voorhees—where ironically they are best known for their coffee—I will attempt to be officially recognized as *competent*. As humbling moments go, it's a humble one, yet I hope to be up for the task.

Yes, my fellow readers and writers, I am a member of Toastmasters International. Tonight, right after I deliver and get evaluated on my tenth official speech, I will have the opportunity to apply for my free Competent Communicator (CC) Award. I suspect that I will display the framed certificate prominently in my housc just in casc my wife and other would-be doubters have arrived at the opinion that I am completely inept, incapable, and, yes, incompetent.

Upon joining Toastmasters, I was given two manuals—*Competent Leadership (CL),* and *Competent Communication (CC).* My instant spin was that I, and the other newbies (in addition to the few people worldwide who haven't sought fit to join this venerable group yet), were being labeled as incompetents. It was a kick to my solar plexus and my ego, but I have soldiered on—as I also appreciated the opportunity to achieve competency by simply preparing and delivering ten short speeches in front of a crowd (and over the whirring of espresso machines) of mostly fellow incompetents.

Looking back upon my almost completed journey to competence, it seems that I have taken a circuitous route and I'd like to share some of those scenes with you.

Scene one: It has been documented in the minds of my family that right out of the womb I began to cry. Legend has it that my first cry was a spirited one, bellowed out as if I were a dog whose joystick was squished by an NFL lineman. Healthy lungs or not, the moment apparently was greeted warmly by my parents and the medical practitioners in attendance. Amidst all the euphoria and bedlam, I received no evaluation of my first cry, and I was left to wonder how well I communicated my entry into this world. I have since read that it's not healthy to go through life with such uncertainty, and I wish that there had been an official Toastmasters evaluator there to comment on my efficacy. Actually, my dad had been an active Toastmaster in his University of Minnesota days, but did not think to bring his CC manual with him. Perhaps he lost some CL points, as well as some sleep as a result.

Scene two: Tired of simply crying, wailing, and bawling my way through life, at six months or so, I started to speak, although I can't remember if I had prepared my remarks or done so extemporaneously. I do recall my first four words and expressions to be the following:

1. Ma-Ma
2. Da-Da
3. Ma-Ma, Da-Da

4. I am desirous of some nutritional sustenance, preferably emanating from Ma-Ma's mammary glands.

I recall my first three utterances being greeted by smiles and congratulatory embraces. After the fourth, for some reason Ma-Ma and Da-Da (I'm not sure if my older brothers were present) fainted on the hardwood floor. This kind of sucked, as my main sources of nutritional sustenance were now disabled for several hours.

I've often wondered what would have happened if prior to fainting (or even afterward), my parents had seen fit to praise me for the competence of my word construction. Oh sure, they loved me, otherwise praised me, and sacrificed plenty for me, but they never greeted me with that all-important c-word. If only they dared to give me that dream.

Scene three: We fast-forward to my second-grade classroom at Beth El (day school) in Camden, New Jersey. A major part of competent communication, to me, is the ability to make friends, or at least make conversational wisecracks during class. If memory serves, I had a friend in second grade named Larry Sragow (what's up, Larry, if you're reading this), and while I was still a shy boy in many respects, I was working at mastering my ability to talk during class and still concentrate enough on the lessons presented to garner good grades.

Enter the infamous Ms. Lutek, the most sadistic second-grade teacher this side of, of … okay, *the* most sadistic second grade school teacher in the recorded universe. Ms. Lutek once did not take kindly to a classmate asking her a couple times what time "phys ed" started, so while the rest of the class went to phys ed, the offending student spent the period in Ms. Lutek's room standing up at her desk while holding a trash can. Ms. Lutek was not a big fan of my talking to Larry and the other kids, and she would repeatedly have me stand in the back corner of the classroom—in a semidark triangular area—for hours at a time. I'm still not sure what these episodes did to my psyche, my metabolism, my feelings of competence, and my ability to perform with German girls over the years. I was grateful to go to public school the next year.

Scene four: In fourth-grade class (or was it fifth?), we actually shot a little movie with whatever technology was at hand. I was the male lead in a short film based on Saki's *The Open Window*, and I played the part of Mr. Nuttle. I don't remember getting any rave reviews—let alone anyone getting carried away and calling me "competent." What I do remember is having my picture on the front page of the *Progress Press*, alongside fellow movie star Janet Lazowski. Now, the *Progress Press* was a biweekly, eight-page rag, and not particularly competent even by the usual standards of biweekly, eight-page municipal rags. Still, it beat standing in the back of Ms. Lutek's prison cell with my mouth taped while holding a metal trash can.

Scene five: I am standing near the front of my high school graduation line on a hot June day in Medford, New Jersey. As class vice president of Lenape High, I am about to present our class gift, a wooden Indian, which is an homage to our politically incorrect class mascot, and perhaps a snide reference to the personality of most of the teachers there. We didn't actually have a wooden Indian to present, and I remember carrying a little wooden stick with me to the podium, while trying to remember what I had started preparing to say while standing in line. I recall delivering it with some semblance of competence and getting obligatory applause and even a little laughter from those who got my humor.

I had been voted senior class veep, which was really the consolation prize for finishing second in the presidential race, where there may have been ten or so of us who ran. I'm ever grateful that I didn't win, as it would have required my actually doing something more than stepping to a podium on a hot June day with a stick in my hand. What was the platform of my campaign, and the theme of my almost-winning speech? Utilizing my initials, it was "MJG: More Jews in Government." Exit polls showed that I captured 88 percent of the Jewish vote, but alas, we comprised only 5 percent of my senior class.

Scene six: Off to college at the University of Pennsylvania, where I enrolled in easy classes, and proceeded to throw away easy grades by never attending said classes. (In all fairness, I sometimes showed up for exams.) Socially, I was somewhat popular within my circle—intramural jock meets semidrunk druggie meets practical intellectual wiseass—and would probably be remembered by other inhabitants of this circle for displaying a strong vocabulary within the accepted tableau of irreverent profanity. There were no awards or certificates to be had for such achievement, but the experiences increased my confidence level in a strange manner.

Scene seven: The twenty-plus (ouch!) years since college have been a blur, and in those years, I have held, lost, and quit good and bad jobs in a variety of arenas—mostly social service, teaching, and sales. While I certainly don't possess an awe-inspiring resume, I have had the opportunity to give dozens or possibly hundreds of presentations and even a TV appearance or two. My guesstimate is that I have prepared adequately for about half of them and reactions to my speeches have ranged from excitement and rapt attention to indifference and even antipathy. To my knowledge, I've never been booed off a stage or podium, nor was I ever asked for my autograph or thrown a pair of panties or a hotel room key afterwards. (Perhaps I'm now repressing the reactions I was greeted with during a speech to the Teamsters Union.)

Scene eight: Seeing an ad for the local chapter of Toastmasters International, I respond and then attend my first meeting last year. I befriend, in a loose kind of way, a young couple who are also first-time guests, and within a week or two we all take the plunge together, pay our dues, and face up to our incompetence. Toastmasters is a little like Alcoholics Anonymous, but it's only a ten-step program—each step (speech) to be completed on our own schedule. To keep our dignity, we don't stand up and say, 'Hi, I'm Matt G, and I'm an incompetent speaker," nor do the commingled competents and incompetents say, "Welcome, Matt" (and not only to avoid the pun). In so joining, I felt that I was fulfilling an unspoken promise, or at least paying a little tribute, to my dad, who still speaks glowingly—and I daresay *competently*—about his experiences there.

Of my other nine formal speeches, I would say that I had outlined two of them with more than twelve hours to go before show time. My tenth and final one will be like the other seven, as I will prepare an outline using some of the contents of this column and, if I'm lucky, will complete the outline an hour before the start of the meeting. In fact, the speech I probably prepared the best for was titled, "Procrastination: I'll Tell You All About it Later." It was a speech of, by, and about procrastination, and it still made me feel a little like that skinny, long-haired, almost eighteen-year-old carrying the wooden stick to my graduation podium.

This feeling, which I will experience in exactly six hours, has me asking the following question: Have I been a competent communicator all along, or is it simply impossible to teach me *anything* new?

MJG's note: Call me a *dumbass* if you will, but I just found out that the noisy thing that I had always been calling an "expresso" machine is really an "espresso" machine. I had to edit that, lest you think I am totally incompetent. My excuse: I don't drink anything coffee-related, unless you consider hot chocolate (a quick plug: the hot chocolate at Wawa is awesome) a distant relative.

My speech to Toastmasters? It was well received and I also received my Toastmasters International Competent Communicator award. I would display it prominently, but I haven't framed it yet. My award leans against a stack of books, somewhere in my home office from where I'm now communicating with you.

Question: Does laziness cancel out competence, or can they peacefully coexist?

Ruprecht and Roddy: A Father's Day Tale of Sorts

June 2009

As Father Day approaches, I'm grateful that my own dad—whom I was able to pay tribute to in this space one year ago—is still a pillar in my life. While our opinions and tastes were certainly not always in lockstep with one another as I was growing up, I never had to second-guess Dad's love and stabilizing presence. Truly, I could always take those things for granted, which didn't keep me from complaining about his imperfections, as I saw them. I'm very resourceful that way.

Many birthdays later, I try to be there for him, hoping that we will have many more Father's Days together, but knowing that each new one is to be cherished. This all has me thinking about a strange story I heard about a septuagenarian who was able to meet his father for the very first time. He may have even been a *vegetarian septuagenarian*, but my brain started hurting after the first ten syllables of such description. Truth be told, I dozed off during the story, so I had to imagine their dialogue. Ever grateful that the following is not autobiographical (and not only because I don't want to age myself another thirty years), here are the details of their meeting.

Through some combination of dogged persistence, cosmic realignment, and pure dumb luck, a man meets up with his long-lost father. We pick up the conversation as this man, Ruprecht, a spry gent of seventy-eight years, regards his dad, Roderick, with a look of bewilderment. Roderick, a month short of hitting the century mark, is still a very handsome and dapper *dude about town*. He enjoys almost everything in life but being called "Roddy."

"So," Ruprecht begins with a conjunction, "what's going on, D—?" He stops in midword and rather awkwardly extends his hand. Feeling a bit conflicted about the whole thing, his handshake is one of those dreaded dead mackerels.

Roderick recoils from the squishy shake and then manages to say, "I'm okay, Ruprecht. You know, it's great to see you, son. You wanna grab a bite to eat? On me? That's the least I can do."

"That *is* the least you can do. But no, I always have my big meal at noon. I'm not really hungry."

"Ruprecht, why do you eat your big meal so early?"

"Um, it's healthier. That's what my doctor tells me."

"Your doctor? You listen to him? What does he know?"

"Um, he's a she." (One can tell that Roderick's not a big fan of the *ums*.) "Doctor Katrina. And not only she says it; everyone agrees."

"Okay, so what does *she* know? I've been stuffing myself late at night for as long as I can remember, and look at me. (He beats on his chest proudly, a la Tarzan.) "I'm gonna be one hundred next month, you know. Son," he continues, not catching the irony, "did I raise you to eat a lousy dinner?"

"Um, well, Roddy, you really didn't raise me at all. And your diet is not what works for me."

Boy, you youngsters are so obstinate. You always were such a stub—." He stops himself. "Hey, Ruprecht, you know my lady friend is planning a big shindig for my one—"

"Your *lady friend*?!"

"Yeah, that's right. Her name's Dottie. She's a lovely dame. Out of respect to your mom, I didn't get serious with her until last year." It's BS and irrelevant, but he thought he'd smooth it over a bit.

"Well, that's considerate of you," Ruprecht says agreeably enough.

"Thank you. Anyway, as I was saying, Dottie's planning a one hundredth party for me next month, and we'd love to have ya."

"Ah, I don't know. I'd feel like I was crashing or something."

"Hey, fuggetabout it." Roderick always liked to stay almost relevant in a pop culture kind of way. "You're family, right? What's your phone number? I'll text you."

"I don't text."

"Do you phone?"

"Yeah, I phone." Ruprecht can't help but admire his dad's persistence here. "It's 555-547-2368."

"Terrific. So, Ruprecht, what do you say we catch some dinner together? There's a great place right down the street—Lugo's. I'll eat heavy and you can eat light if you prefer."

"Well, maybe I'll take you up on your offer. You know, just thinking about it, I'm getting hungrier."

"Now you're talking, Rupe. Atta guy!" He gives him a good-natured, hearty pat on the back. "Can I ask you something? What was up with that limp-wristed handshake you gave me earlier?"

"I'll explain it, if you tell me what was up with that first name you gave me?"

"What's wrong with Ruprecht?! That was my big brother's name. Still is. Big, strong guy. Runs a pig farm in Montana. Now when he shakes your hand, you can feel it in your toes."

"I hate my name, Dad. Regardless of my celebrity uncle, the pig farmer, and all the sentimentality attached to that. There are not even any cool nicknames for Ruprecht and my ex-wife also detested my name."

"Congratulations, son. I didn't know you got married."

"Dad, I've been divorced for thirty-seven years."

"That's why we need to catch up more often, son. Starting with dinner at Lugo's."

"Sure, whatever. Say, do they serve a good burger at Lugo's?"

"The best. They have an All-Things-Lugo Burger that is amazing. When you bite into it, you can—"

"Feel it in your toes?"

"How'd you guess? Took you awhile, Rupe, but you're starting to catch on." He gives his son an even heartier pat on the back—a toe-curdling pat that almost floors him.

MJG's note: I'm not sure what happens next with Ruprecht and Roderick, but I hope that they will enjoy some more moments together, including Dottie's big shindig. As for me, I look forward to my dinner with Dad and, among other things, watching him hold my growing baby. While he enjoys my visits and phone calls, he absolutely lights up whenever he sees and hears Baby Benny, who is also similarly moved by the presence of Grandpa (*Yei-yei*, to him).

And did I mention that my dad still comes through with the type of hearty handshake that makes even my toes smile?

Books by the (Baker's) Dozen

July 2009

My wife Ruby, a voracious reader, often asks me why I don't read more. In truth, she makes a good point. During most of the ten years she's known me—with rare exception—I've been neither an ardent reader nor a prolific writer. I *have* been a most voracious, even rapacious, eater and TV viewer on her watch, qualities that haven't impressed her greatly. Go figure.

Since becoming the parents of Baby Ben last July, she has done her best to try to get me to shut off the boob tube and pick up more books. Again, she is onto something here; whenever the TV is on around Ben, he stops what he's doing and becomes transfixed by whatever emanates from the screen. So if done on my watch (and his), he has viewed a lot of games, some news, a little *Seinfeld* and other classic sitcoms, and bits and pieces of a movie or two. I'm not sure how much these TV sessions will either aid or impede his growth, but I do share Ruby's wish that our boy become an avid reader. And from my perspective anyway, if he achieves this while also getting to love the Phillies, the Eagles, Rafael Nadal, Tiger Woods, and, um, Ralph Kramden and Marion Cotillard, so much the better.

But, back to books. I *have* been trying to read more of late, whether out loud to Ben or just for my own sense of enjoyment and edification—these two categories don't have to be mutually exclusive, or mutually inclusive, for that matter. In fact, I've polished off a book or two in the last couple or so weeks, and thought I'd share some quickie reviews of thirteen of them. As an added service, I've also included Baby Ben's analysis.

1. ***The Cat in the Hat* by Dr. Seuss, (61 pages)**

Review: A mischievous cat magically appears in the home of "little boy," Sally, and their worrywart fish on a rainy day when they're stuck inside the house. Hilarity and great rhymes ensue, complemented by amusing drawings. Still awesome after all these years!
My Rating: 9.5 out of 10
Baby Ben's Take: Thing One and Thing Two are cool, and I liked the fish in the pot.

2. ***Curious George and the Firefighters* by Margret and H.A. Rey, –(23 un-numbered pages)**

Review: A hyperactive, highly distractible primate goes with a school group on a field trip to the firehouse, accompanies the firemen on a job, and ends up juggling for a nervous crowd as the men save a pizza parlor from the blaze. Decent writing and art work. Does anyone still use the term "pizza parlor?"
My Rating: **7**
Baby Ben's Take: I like the big size of the book, and I try to rip out the pages before Daddy stops me.

3. ***Eight Animals Bake A Cake* by Susan Middleton Elya and Lee Chapman (29 unnumbered pages)**

Review: A fun story and a nice introduction to the Spanish language. Good, vivid pictures, and rendered with a nice sense of humor.
My Rating: 8
Baby Ben's Take: Very unrealistic; I can see eight animals eating a cake, but baking it? However, *me gusto el gato.* Daddy's command of Spanish needs work.

4. ***Falling Up* by Shel Silverstein– (171 pages)**

Review: I had never read Shel before, and this book has a lot of poems that work on at least two levels. Alternately corny, witty, and sneakily subversive, with whimsical black-and-white sketches. A good read for kids and adults—and babies?
My Rating: 8
Baby Ben's Take: Not a big fan of the black-and-white, but that's cool. Me gusto the rhymes. I just found out that Shel wrote, "A Boy Named Sue," the old Johnny Cash hit.

5. ***Fox in Sox* by Dr. Seuss –(61 pages)**

Review: Tongue-twisting torment—and heaven. Fun to read out loud, even if I get tripped up more than the Knox character.
My Rating: 9.5
Baby Ben's Take: I enjoy Knox's linguistic and physical revenge on Fox. Gives me ideas.

6. ***Franklin and the Hero* by Paulette Bourgeois and Brenda Clark–(10 power-packed pages in a pillow book format)**

Review: The eponymous turtle and his best friend, Snail, realize that by doing little things to help people, they can become heroes just like their own idol, Dynaroo. Got it? A pretty good, touching read that causes a tear or two to flow.
My Rating: 7.5
Baby Ben's Take: Daddy's voice sounds the same whether he's doing Mrs. Muskrat or Dynaroo. Makes it confusing. I do like that the book doubles as a pillow—comes in handy!

7. ***Hickory, Dickory, Dock and Other Favorite Nursery Rhymes* illustrated by Sonja Rescek (19 un-numbered pages)**

Review: A fun read-aloud of purportedly classic sing-song rhymes that have been around forever. The art work is decent. Observation: some of these rhymes from bygone times are incredibly stupid and many are kind of mean-spirited. I do, however, enjoy patting Ben during Pat-a-Cake.
My Rating: 7
Baby Ben's Take: Meh ... some of these are kind of stupid. I kind of enjoy Pat-a-Cake, but instead of hitting me, why doesn't Daddy just give me a cake? I mean, if the eight animals can enjoy one ...

8. ***Is Your Mama a Llama?* By Deborah Guarino and Steven Kellogg (27 un-numbered pages)**

Review: A curious llama, presumably not named George, asks each of his friends, "Is your mama a llama?" and they respond in turn with a rhyming description of their mothers. It's your basic, entertaining llama melodrama.
My Rating: 7.5
Baby Ben's Take: Couldn't they find something to rhyme with pelican?

9. ***Louis the Fish* by Arthur Yorinks and Richard Egielski (29 un-numbered pages)**

Review: I once ran a volunteer-based, read-aloud program and discovered this gem of a book. It became my favorite, as it's actually witty and funny with terrific art work to match the great writing. In brief, Louis has been surrounded by meat since birth, and becomes a third-generation butcher by default and circumstance. In his spare time, he seeks out, draws, and dreams about fish, until ... (I won't spoil it further).
My Rating: 9.5
Baby Ben's Take: When Daddy rediscovered this book, he became almost as excited as when the Phillies won the World Series. Gotta give him props for this one—pretty cool stuff.

10. ***Oink* published by Barron's Educational Services (10 un-numbered pages)**

Review: Your garden variety children's book. Kills a minute or two with decent art work to enjoy. No great joy here.
My Rating: 5.5

Baby Ben's Take: First-rate investigative journalism! A fascinating expose of the culinary preferences of barnyard animals.

11. ***A Prayer For Owen Meany* by John Irving (543 pages)**

Review: Irving is a very popular and highly acclaimed author of titles including *The World According to Garp* and *The Cider House Rules.* I had never read him before but am glad I took on this long novel. Owen Meany is a unique, surreal character and this book touches upon many themes along the way, including fate and determinism, faith, family relationships, and the Vietnam War from the perspective of twenty years later (the story takes place about twenty years ago). The nonlinear storytelling and political commentary didn't always work for me, but the book was compelling, and the writing top-notch. The conclusion was a little less than satisfying for me.
My Rating: 8
Baby Ben's Take: Geez, I thought he would never finish this book. He never read it aloud to me, and I can see why. I did leaf through it a little, and thought that the political commentary was quite on-point, and the ending seemed to be very satisfying—in the sense that it concluded.

12. ***Thomas the Tank Engine: Shapes and Sizes* published by Random House (10 un-numbered pages)**

Review: Just a crappy little nothing book by the huge Thomas the Tank Engine empire, which I was introduced to time and time again by our four-year-old nephew. I've, alas, become a reluctant fan of Thomas,

even as I rue all the money we may end up spending on *Thomas and Friends*, if Ben becomes hooked on it. But this book has poor, lazy drawings and is crappy—even by crappy-little-nothing-book standards.
Rating: 3 (being generous)
Baby Ben's Take: A lousy little book, but I think I'm hooked on the concept. Mommy and Daddy took me to see a Thomas display at Barnes and Noble the other night. Did I mention that I think I'm hooked?

13. ***The Wolf Who Cried Boy*** **by Bob Hartman and Tim Raglin (27 un-numbered pages)**

Review: So, going alphabetically, we end up saving the best for last! This is a marvelous parody of "The Boy Who Cried Wolf," and it teaches the same lesson. What could have been a lazy little play on words is a brilliantly executed story. Witty, funny, with perfect artwork that elevates it to the highest level. A great surprise for me.
Rating: 10
Baby Ben's Take: Why did the little wolf complain about eating lamburgers and sloppy does? Sounded pretty good to me. I get a lot of milk and blended fruit and the occasional slurp of soup. I can't sympathize with this ungrateful, devious wolf who wants to eat little boys. Of all things! But since my dad continues to read it to me, I'll have to learn to endure it. Maybe I'll rip out the pages.

Well, there you have it, friends: an eclectic summer reading list of sorts. Happy reading to all, and to all some good reads.

Mixed Emotions and Great Neanderthal Poetry

August 2009

Roses are red
Violets are blue
I hate silly poems
So here's a haiku:

Finding the wrong words
For my unfinished essay
A great new poem

As my haiku attests, I have something of a love-contempt relationship with poetry. At its most mediocre, much of the poetry I have experienced has one too many of these qualities:

- It's self-obsessive—if you don't believe me, try to sit through a local poetry reading
- It's half-baked
- As written or recited/performed, the writer has given me no compelling reason to enter his/her world

In the intro to my own book of poetry, in which, hopefully, very few of my fifty-two eclectic poems contain one or more of these elements, I utilize a quote from a musician/writer named John Cage: "I have nothing to say, and I am saying it, and that is poetry." Cage's statement accounts for half of my sentiments toward poetry. Did I mention that my book is titled, *Mixed Emotions: Poetry for the Open-Minded*? It is ...

On the other hand (I guess you knew that there had to be another hand), poetry is the greatest medium to express the written word for the following reasons—and more:

- Do you remember the tagline for Outback Steakhouse? "No rules, just right." Poetry embodies that slogan for me. If you know the basic rules of your language, feel free to bend and break them in the service of a good poem. Freedom of expression is the essence of good poetry. Yes, it can be employed in prose as well, but have you ever heard the expression "prosaic license?" Didn't think so.
- I can't play music, and God (along with some would-be partners who either had their toes bruised or were too embarrassed to be seen on the dance floor with me) knows that I have no rhythm as a dancer, yet I can use words quite rhythmically. When I'm in my poetic zone, words sing and dance and soar in ways that I otherwise couldn't hope to approximate.
- There must be a reason that everything from a brilliant sunset to Dr. J in his prime swooping his way to the basket is said to be

poetic or *poetry in motion.* The reason is that poetry at its best is majestic, elevating ideas and emotions to the highest of levels.

- There are so many different types of poems. Rhyming and nonrhyming. Ballads and elegies. Epics and odes. Haiku and limericks. There's just gotta be a style to read or write poetry that suits you. To say that I hate poetry because so much of it can be self-obsessive, half-baked, and arcane would be like disavowing all music because I've heard hundreds of *crap-o-licious* songs in a row.

With a newfound enthusiasm for poetry, I asked my crack—or only slightly cracked—research team to look into the history of poetry. What they found was reason enough for this sometimes ambivalent Jewish poet to crack a prideful smile. Let me share this with all of you, even if you're nonambivalent, non-Jewish, and nonpoetic.

A little known fact: the very first poem ever written has been credited to a legendary Jewish poet named Sheldon "Big Stones" Firestein. Scientists and *poetologists* believe that Firestein lived about 32,000 years ago. After furious scholarly debate, there is general agreement that Firestein lived in one of two places—in a land mass now known as Zagreb, Croatia, or near a shopping mall in Paramus, New Jersey. But, exact location aside, this much is known about old Big Stones:

- Sheldon stood about 168 cm tall, or roughly 5'6", with the cranial capacity of at least two average Neanderthals.
- He was a fierce hunter and fighter, but found time to do a little tutoring on the side.

- Sheldon always regretted that he couldn't keep kosher, sometimes castigating himself in his writings. He was said to have invented a very tasty gefilte fish with pigs knuckles dish, which apparently became all the rage in Zagreb—or was it Paramus?
- He was founder and first director of the Pleistocene Poets League (PPL), which met in a secret cave, yet still boasted an average of at least twenty attendees at their Tuesday night meetings.
- Firestein was said to have died after challenging a heckler to step outside after a Tuesday night meeting. Apparently, seventeen members of the audience took him up on his challenge, and it took all of them to subdue Firestein. Paleontologists have discovered what looked to be the remnants of fourteen wooden spears embedded in his sternum. On a happier note, this incident was a springboard for banning all wooden and stone weaponry from all future meetings of the PPL, which somehow continued in his absence.

But I digress. Let's get to a few examples of Firestein's poetry, which have been assiduously translated into Modern English without losing the flavor of the original.

Speaking about the dangers of premarital sex, the Pleistocene Poet warned the youth of his town in a poem titled *Don't Do It, Boneheads.*

Ooga, wooga, booga
Fooga, nooga, tooga
Ba wa pa, na wa ja
Sooga, Hooga, Kooga.

While some of the meaning may be lost today, one can still appreciate his passion, rhythm, and ironic word play. Not content to simply write rhyming poetry, Sheldon tried his hand at some free verse in his seminal poem, *Losing My Stone Marbles.*

Once upon a late night dreary
Ooga Ba, Wa Na Tumpi
Kaba Dega Fa Fa Fa
Oy vey, I'm going meshugge.

I am always overwhelmed by the pure emotion and self-awareness of this poem. Yet, it is Firestein's haiku—a form that he was just developing before his tragic murder—that has me scratching my head in amazement. Let me share three examples of his haiku, which the master did not title. He apparently felt that the words should speak for themselves, and how they did!

Va va va va voom
Pig and bison light my fire
Synagogue awaits

...

Awake my good men
Before slaying that huge beast
Read them poetry

...

Looking out my cave
Crows and eagles fill the sky
I'm getting shpilkes

By the way, the closest definition I can provide for *shpilkes* is "a state of great nervousness or anxiety." Like cholesterol and emotions in general, there is *good shpilkes* and *bad shpilkes.* And I think that this is appropriate for my discussion of poetry and the emotions it inspires.

Lest the lessons of Sheldon "Big Stones" Firestein be lost, I hope that many of you will continue to read and write poetry that inspires *good shpilkes*. In fact, whatever your style of writing, express it in such a way that the reader or listener is compelled to enter your world. Share with us your full palate of ideas and emotions, but don't give us mixed emotions about entering it in the first place. If you can do that, just know that somewhere Firestein is smiling and might be inspired to writc something like this:

Lyrical writing
Fills my soul like bison soup
My heart is busting

All That Twitters Is Not Goldberg

September/October 2009

My Phellow Philistines, or is it Philly-stines (nah),
My Lovable Luddites (take three),
My Honorable Hittites (looks more alliterative than it sounds),

Hey Hittites,

Last Wednesday was one of those 90/90/100 early evenings that I so dread. As I was mowing my lawn with my rotary lawnmower—more on that in just a sec—I knew that it was at least 90 degrees, with 90-plus percent humidity, and a 100 percent chance that I would abandon the project before completion. If I could afford a sauna, I would have surely jumped in it to cool off.

Just prior to mowing, I watched a quasi-news show on ESPN, and saw a feature about athletes and their use of Twitter. At the time, I had never used Twitter, and had no desire to learn enough about it to justify my hatred. I did know that Twitter was one of those horrific social networking sites that I have tried to avoid, because: 1) I avoid most new things; 2) I'm a nice enough guy, but only quasi-social; 3) I hate the whole "Will you be my friend?" world, and all of the "Will you be my Valentine?" BS it connotes; and 4) I have enough real friends without acquiring all these virtual ones, and if I do start playing this game, my ultracompetitive demons may descend on all my friends—my five real ones and my 2,347,892 fake ones alike.

The feature talked about the scads of athletes who tweet (post a message of some degree of great urgency on Twitter). There was one NFL player who was caught tweeting during games. Another has talked openly about tweeting after scoring a touchdown. NFL fans may recall that the TD celebration has featured all kinds of individual and team antics over the years, but was ushered into the modern age when psycho-celeb Terrell (TO) Owens pulled a Sharpie out of his sock and signed a football. Not old school, but clever enough. Trying to outdo TO, fellow wide receiver and showman Joe Horn hid a cell phone in the goalpost turnbuckle, and pulled it out to call home (?) after he scored. The post-TD tweet would just be part of a natural evolution or devolution, wouldn't it?

Where exactly is this world heading, I asked my nontechno self, as I struggled to push my little green mower up the small inclines of my front yard. It wasn't lost on me that I was using this old-fashioned machine not by choice, but because I couldn't keep a real mower running properly. I never got the oil/gas combo right on my gas mowers, or when I did, the blades would get broken because of all the sticks and rocks I ran over. The electric mower I bought ran okay, but it kept shutting off the circuit breakers, so I exchanged it for one more gas mower, before giving up and trying the centuries-proven technology.

After a few minutes of pushing—cutting through the high grass with this mower was like trying to cut a diamond with a toothpick—I fulfilled my prophecy and gave up. But during my thirty minutes or so of actual mowing, I took inventory of myself and how I felt that I fit into this new world.

I may have refused most of the friend invites I got from people—and sometimes, they were sent by actual friends—to join sites such as Plaxo, hi5, and LinkedIn, but a little piece of me actually wanted to be part of this whole world of self-promotion. It's just that things always went wrong when I tried to join the online party. An old friend from college sent me an invitation to join hi5, so I replied, completing my registration, and ... nothing blew up immediately. So far, so good!

The problem was that I had inadvertently done something that sent everyone in my address book invitations to join hi5. People I hadn't heard from in years were sending me "thanks, but no thanks" e-mails. After either the third or fifteenth one, I figured out why they were e-mailing me, but was still dumbfounded as to how I had sent them invitations in the first place. So, being the slightly anal guy that I am 66.345 percent of the time, I sent everyone in my large address book individual e-mails to apologize for disrupting their peace and cyber-quiet. Apologies accomplished, I then sent my erstwhile friend a slightly peeved e-mail, blaming her for setting off this chain reaction. I reacted as if she had purchased me a Trojan horse. Or a gas lawnmower.

Outside of the social networking sites (and some quick research showed that there are hundreds of them with billions of subscribers between them), I'm not a total Hittite. With apologies to those who I am addressing, I confess that I am addicted to e-mail and couldn't live without it—or my cell phone for that matter. Having said that, this puts me at least three paradigm shifts behind current communication systems, and I still don't text. Oh sure, I could easily get addicted to texting if either of the following were true: 1) I had a usage plan that didn't cost me fifteen cents every time I read or sent some useless communiqué, and 2) I had a real keyboard on my phone that allowed me to type more than seven words per hour. Absent both of those prerequisites, I guess I'll keep on hating *text-world*.

One quick footnote to my texting experience: A gifted, young, motivational speaker from my Toastmasters chapter had moved about an hour away and I missed seeing him at our meetings. He didn't reply to the couple e-mails I sent his way, but I did start receiving these supposedly motivational truisms on my cell phone. It took me awhile to realize who they were coming from, and it upset me because I get more than enough e-mails of this variety, but at least they don't cost me to read them.

I finally did the unthinkable and texted him back to stop sending me this, um, crap that I had to pay for. I'm not a bad guy, and neither is he, and I'd gladly take him out for a beer, or lunch, and spend twenty times what I was paying to receive his techno-wisdom. To be truthful, I will also tell you that my reply to him was strongly worded, but some of my peevish momentum had been lost in its transmission. It is hard to be forceful when you feel like you're typing with crayons.

So what about Twitter? Did I secretly yearn to be part of this world, when I had passed on MySpace and Facebook, and Lord knows what other faddish sites along the way? It irked me to high heaven that 1) I didn't even know much about Twitter, and 2) that I was mixing metaphors in the process of being irked. So I decided to venture once more into uncharted territory and experience a little of what I had been missing. I mean, every TV and radio show seemed to be soliciting tweets, and as much as I hated the trend, thought it only fair to look my hatred into the gut and see what other metaphors I could scramble.

The registration was easy enough, as I'm a reasonably fast typist when not using a cell phone or laptop. It cost nothing, and I didn't even have to reply to an e-mail in order to join. I'll get around to reading the terms of usage next year, but I cleverly avoided sending everyone in my address book my proclamation that I had joined over 25,000,000 _____ (twits?...twats?) who tweeted. I soon found a directory—which I can't seem to locate now—of the most popular "Tweetmeisters."

In T-Land, instead of fake friends—although they probably have them as well—you can follow others (and get updated every time they tweet), and you can also beg, borrow, or steal your own followers. As I am writing, I found an unaffiliated Web site called twitterholic.com (I swear that is the only word I made up in this whole paragraph is *Tweetmeister.*) which tracks the top one thousand Twitterholics based on number of followers. I'm not sure what this says about our society, but each person or entity in their top ten—listed here from most to least—had more than 2,000,000 followers:

1. Ashton Kutcher (What, you were expecting a mindless celebrity?)
2. The Ellen (DeGeneres) Show (What, you wanted real talent?)
3. Britney Spears (That's more like it.)
4. CNN Breaking News (Insert clever comment.)
5. Twitter (Twitter itself ... I don't get it.)
6. Ryan Seacrest (Why not? He's only on TV or radio ten hours a day.)
7. Kim Kardashian (I'll sample and share some of her wisdom in my *Part 2.*)

8. "The Real Shaq" (Shaquille O'Neal's tweets, not done by an unauthorized imposter, but by his real paid publicist.)
9. John Mayer (the musician and chick magnet in his own words)
10. Oprah Winfrey (finishing one spot ahead of a fellow Chicago pal, some guy named Barack Obama)

Seeing the list, I had mixed feelings about forging on, but I set up my profile and then thought about making/doing/authoring my first tweet. As I was about to pound the keyboard, I feared that I would get addicted and need to acquire more followers than President Obama, even as I knew that Kim Kardashian was in a whole other league.

A little research was in order before attempting to publish my first tweet. To make sure there are no wasted letters let alone extra words on ones posts, the Web site restricts all such entries to 140 characters, including punctuation marks and spaces. Another nice feature is that with each keystroke, the 140 counts down. Feeling the pressure of making the perfect tweet, I decided to find out why Ashton Kutcher has so many followers (okay, he's good looking, married to a famous older woman, and has a built-in following from TV and movies). But he also must be one hell of a writer, right? Let's see:

The man with 3.4 million followers as of September 2, 2009 is apparently a big fantasy football fan. He also lived up to his reputation for *pranking and punking*, tweeting this entry: **"haaaaaaaaachoooooooooo,"** which linked his followers to a YouTube video showing slow-motion sneezes played to an operatic soundtrack. In fact, including the linked address, this total tweet only used up forty-two characters. The guy is good; no wonder why Demi Moore is so in love.

The pressure was on to try to post something at an Ashtonian level—incisive, funny, cutting edge, and well within 140, as no doubt all of his 3.4 million minions were very busy people. After wracking my brain harder than I do when writing one of these columns, I finally came up with this: **"Hey people, I'm sitting here in shorts and a t-shirt talking to you all. Weather's cool, and so are you for reading this. That's all folks!"**

Not a terrible first entry, but more research was needed. I went to #2, the Ellen DeGeneres Show. Her page also brings in more than 3 million people (I refuse to use the tragically hip word, "tweeple," a term I just picked up from Oprah's page), and all she really does—from what I can tell—is plug her talk show. Judging by her first couple of pages, she doesn't respond to her followers; she simply tells us what's on her show. Here's a recent tweet of Ellen's: **"shine a light on the sm businesses that make a diff in your community. Join nbc, amex & other business owners like me & nominate 2today!"**

Not bad. She used 138 coveted spots and even combined *2today* to not risk going over the limit. (I am still trying to decipher what an "sm business is," and am wondering if the "&" was left out to save space.) I studied her post. Could I possibly match Ellen's overall brilliance? Not sure. Oh, I could probably get my own syndicated TV show, and I have married a pretty woman like Ellen has, but to achieve that level of sophistication in my writing? Not in this lifetime.

Still not ready to sound my own tweet, I went over to the Britney Spears page. From what I can tell, Brit the Twit's MO is to reply to some of her idolaters—à la Ashton—and send links to her concert photos, contests, and the like. Her writing, to say nothing of her body these days, is as tight as Hemingway's, and the latter inspires commentary from her gushing fans, like this entry: **"I are so cool Britney!!! :P"** (And, you thought good grammar was a thing of the past.) Another was moved to write, and I cut and paste, **"i heart you! :D**

Trust me, I am trying to coexist in this crazy-cool world, but I can't even begin to tell you all the ways that this latest (just sixteen characters used) post turned my tummy. As for Brit, she's looking good again, but I'm too modest to walk around with a flat stomach, and have some unknown people *hearting* me. It's bad enough being hearted by people I know.

I couldn't wait any longer, and I decided to stop by the Twitter page of the young woman who has more followers than all but six people and networks in the known universe—Kim Kardashian. From what I recall, Kim is the daughter of one of OJ Simpson's attorneys (the infamous *Juice* is her godfather), and appeared, or appears, on a reality show featuring the antics of her super-cool, dysfunctional Hollywood family. I think that's close to the pin. But let's be clear: Kim is famous for two things. She's hot, and she knows that she's hot.

I thought that KK, the essence of hotness, would operate under the assumption that we would want to see as many scantily clad pictures of her as humanly possible, and she would offer some very shallow beauty tips or the like. Boy, was I mistaken! Okay, in fairness, she did post a picture of herself with stepbrother, Brody Jenner, at a birthday party. I learned that KK's mom divorced her father (who's now deceased) and married former gold medal decathlete Bruce Jenner. The picture she posted of the two of them had one follower almost drooling the following: **"OMG! you're both way too georgeous people! it should be a crime. x) love you bothhhhhh♥"**

Feeling certain that such a bright fan would not misspell "gorgeous," I still wonder what the true meaning of "georgeous" is. Be that as it may, I discovered that Kim puts a lot of thought into her tweets, quoting from famous people like Dr. Seuss and updating her celeb-obsessed fans on current events, such as this urgent tweet: **"I'm baking a coffee cake right now! yummy!"**

So where exactly does one go after Kim Kardashian when he still isn't ready to post? I had to check in with my dear friend, Sarah Palin, once and former governor of Alaska. Not to be mean, but I thought that "Twitter" was already a contracted nickname for Sarah—a twit, who is a quitter. I was disappointed to see that Palin had a mere 142,000 followers, which was a lot fewer than Brody Jenner had. Adding to that disappointment, as of September 2, 2009, Palin had not tweeted since July 26, offering us this touching farewell of sorts: **"Last state twitter. Thank you Alaska! I love you. God bless Alaska. God bless the U.S.A."**

Wow, just eighty-eight perfectly formed characters—with nary a winking emoticon or a "you betcha" to distract us from her message.

Duly impressed, it was now time to hammer out my own message. After wrestling with my conscience, and still unsure as to which one of us won the bout, I decided on the following, which is now printed indelibly on my "MJGwrites" page: **"I'm doing this as a test case; no desire to tweet and be followed, but this is a research project. That may change over time. Stay tuned."**

As I read it now, the grammar is pretty good, although the first sentence is a bit of a run-on, as I am wont to do every now and then, even while tweeting, as you can plainly see. Still, I only used 137 characters, and it *was* all done in the name of research and an experiment that hurt no animals in the process. To this day (until now), I still haven't told anyone that I have a Twitter account, so I was a little surprised and kind of impressed when I immediately received e-mails announcing that I had *earned* my first two followers. This miracle prompted me to re-tweet: **"Am I becoming addicted to something I thought would repulse me? How did I acquire two followers when I never publicized 'mjgwrites?' Scary!"**

It *was* a little scary, and just a little humbling, to have two followers that I may never meet, or vice versa. Scary and humbling though it was, two weeks later, I only had one follower, and wondered what I did to hold onto him/her.

Let me digress: why do 99.3 percent of those receiving awards describe such moments as humbling experiences. Would they rather be humiliated or further humbled by never receiving their much coveted award? Do they truly behave with humility after being elected to a hall of fame or receiving an Oscar?

I really don't get it, and I really don't know what I've gotten myself into by joining Twitter. I'm not addicted yet (after two and a half weeks, I've produced only two tweets, am officially following nobody, and my one follower is some poor schlemiel who probably got lost), yet in the recent past I have gotten addicted to everything ranging from e-mail to YouTube to cell phones. Yes, I may get sucked in.

All of this, my honorable Hittites, has me a little worried, and I may have to reassess how I will fit into this world after all. It is not so far-fetched to envision myself tweeting like a fool, and telling everyone I know to check my page for all sorts of writing updates. Before I know it, I may start posting pictures of my beautiful son, Benjamin, and if my stomach does become flatter than a slightly deflated beach ball, I may need to share those pics as well. I pondered all of these implications just the other day, as I took out my rotary mower and prepared to do battle with the dense vegetation of my backyard. My lawn was now a perfect jungle of laziness, bad technology, and an unusually wet August in my beloved Delaware Valley.

I was thinking about all of the public appearances I could advertise and all of the coffee cake recipes I could share with all of my disciples when the craziest thing happened. Little Green, aka my lawnmower, crumbled under the weight of the terrible task I had asked it to perform. It *may* be fixable, but the job is clearly above my pay grade.

So please don't be surprised if you go to www.twitter.com/mjgwrites, and see the following (exactly 140-character) tweet: **"URGENT: Yo, anyone near CH, NJ know where I can buy an old-fashioned (no gas, no electric) lawnmower for $60 or less? Thanks, followers!!"**

Sincerely,
Your friend (and still a technophobe at heart),
Matt

A Preview of Coming Distractions

November 2009

One of the joys of writing this column is that it enables me to keep my writing and publishing muscles from degenerating into a state of total atrophy. To this date, I have published (only) two books, but in the last several months, I have put together a couple of manuscripts that I hope to have published in some fashion by the end of 2010. That's next year; I better get cracking!

Let me tell you a little about both projects, although please do not treat this as a full-fledged announcement. That will, hopefully, come soon enough in some way, shape, or format.

The first book is a compendium of these very "The Tip of the Goldberg" columns. With just a smidge of editing and a little additional writing, I have linked my twenty-five-plus columns together with a few updates. While my original intention in writing this column was more to pursue a regular (syndicated?) column than it was to provide material for a book, I hope to now accomplish both.

My working title is *All That Twitters Is Not Goldberg: Truthful Humor from a Vindicated Columnist*, and my hope is that someone other than myself will find the mostly irreverent, but sometimes quite serious, musings of a youngish, middle-aged (yeesh!) man who just became a father—one who tends to write about family issues, sports, movies, politics, and whatever else is on his mind—kind of interesting. Yes, and most of the sentences are not as long as the previous.

Since I've already had the pleasure of sharing many of the contents of that book with you on a monthly basis, I want to also give you just a peek into the second new book that I've really been jamming on. It helps to be an insomniac with a day job that I really don't enjoy—one that I'm apparently not that great at or interested in.

I've just completed the first draft of a book that I've tentatively titled *Wordapedia: 250-Plus Wordapods to Learn, Share, and Master.* Essentially, I've brainstormed 250 (plus a few) words and expressions (*wordapods,* I call them) that *should* be, and it's been a blast to put this together. The Wordapedia has definitions, sample sentences and scenarios, fun facts, interviews with people living in my head space, and all kinds of other cool features. I now see this effort as a syndicated feature, as a calendar, as a book, as a way of life ... all of that. If anyone knows a reputable publisher, agent, or publicist, please let me know, as I think this has real potential. Of course, this book/calendar/way of life has only been breathing in my own head so far, but I love its potential.

So what's it all about? The wordapods are taken from all walks of life—cuisine, academia, sports (there's a whole baseball section), religion, sex, bathroom habits, movies, and scientific theorem. Did I leave anything out? The best way to debut this is to just throw one or two out there. Good news: if you like these, there are 248 more somewhat like them; if you don't, there are 248 others that are quite different. Thank you for reading and keep your fingers crossed for me. When I do so, my typing is even worse than usual. I welcome feedback.

Spinal Tapioca

Spinal tapioca (n)—a pudding given to patients to calm them down after their spinal cords have been punctured

Sample Sentence: Susie dreaded going to the hospital for her invasive procedure, but the spinal tapioca seemed to make it all worthwhile.

Observation: Cheryl Bitman, head of Our Lady of Mediocre Health's excellent Post-Surgery Cuisine Department, lists the preferred food items given to patients after various procedures:

Breast reduction surgery—Chicken (dark meat) with parsley potatoes
Gastric bypass—Beef burritos with chili
Hip replacement—Cereal, skim milk, and fruit
Hernia repair—Something light
Knee replacement—Fish sticks and sauerkraut
Laser vision correction—Peas, carrots and candy
Lobotomies—Split pea soup with a side of pasta
Open heart—Leftovers from hernia repair
Rhinoplasty—Limburger cheese and garlic donuts

Rodentistry

Rodentistry (n)—a highly specialized field of medicine concerning the proper dental care of nibbling mammals

You Know What ... ?

I am proud to call Dr. Woodrow Thorenson a friend. "Thorsie" has enjoyed a thriving rodental practice for over twenty years. Below is an excerpt from an interview I conducted with him.

Matt: Dr. Thorenson, who or what are your patients?

Thorsie: I am fortunate to have quite a varied, eclectic clientele. Everything from beavers to muskrats to chipmunks and squirrels. And, my personal favorite, the lemmings. Do you want to know why they are my favorite?

Matt: Okay, I'll bite.

Thorsie: (wincing a little from the pun) You take care of one lemming, and the rest of them just seem to follow. Cuts down on marketing expenses.

Matt: Are there any types of clients you are not too fond of?

Thorsie: Of course. I'm not a great fan of the porcupine. They are very fussy, and dare I say ...

Matt: Prickly?

Thorsie: Bingo. And I must put in a good word for that beautiful animal—the beaver. It's always a pleasure to see a lot of beavers in my waiting room. There is one downside, though.

Matt: Really?

Thorsie: Every beaver I know is a nocturnal creature. It messes up my office hours, and I have to pay a shift differential and overtime to my rodental hygienists and office staff.

Matt: Never thought of that. Dr. Thorenson, do you have any advice for those thinking about a career in rodentistry?

Thorsie: Let me chew on that a moment. Yes, I do. Forty percent of the world's mammal population is rodents, and they really use their teeth, so it's a great field. Just study hard, get a lot of cheap, easy-clean furniture, and get ready to do battle with the insurance companies.

And that was just a tip of "The Tip of the Goldberg."

MJG's note: "Wordapedia" has since evolved into *Wordapodia—Volume One: An Encyclopedia of Real Fake Words.* I also can't seem to type that first word without transposing the "a" and the "p." Not sure what that says about me, or the book.

Eating My Cake and Having It, Too

December, 2009

My Esteemed Readers,

I bet that most of you—no, I daresay each and every one of you—likes to have your cake, and eat it, too. How scandalous! Can you imagine such a thing?

From the moment I entered this planet, I grew up in a household that valued the power of words. My dad was a copyeditor for various newspapers, mostly *The Philadelphia Inquirer*, and he had a keen eye and ear for effective use of our language. He was a stickler of sorts, and most of that *sticklerizing* stuck to me. Mom also exhibited a strong vocabulary, and she also came from a family of compulsive punsters.

Some of these puns were *pun-itive* in nature, and I have continued the tradition of dishing out such *pun-ishment*. I've been told that being with me is like being stuck in a *pun-nal* colony. Some of my puns are so groaningly good that I'm like *Pun-sutawney Phil:* I see the shadow of my own pun, and have to hide my head for six more weeks before springing up again.

But all punning and kidding aside, I also care deeply about the usage of words. I like to see them used correctly, and love when they're used creatively. And when they're used ineffectively, I do the following:

I question, I analyze, I bristle, I take umbrage (I never give umbrage), and I even get *ballistically* angry. I also have problems with expressions that just don't make any sense. Let me share seven of these idiomatic expressions (make that, *idiot-matic* expressions) with you. These are, of course, idiotic expressions that are spoken robotically by everyday *idioms* like you and me.

- **Have Your Cake and Eat It, Too:** The whole idea of having a cake is to eat it, right? What am I missing here? Let's say my wife bakes me a nice chocolate cake for my birthday. After the pomp and candles, I immediately want to start eating it. Does that make me unusually piggish or something? Okay, maybe I'll give her and the others a bite or two, but you get the idea. Consider this dialogue caused by that idiot-matic expression:

So, honey, aren't you going to eat the cake I made you?

Nah.

Why not?

Oh, I don't want to be like those people.

What people?

You know the type that has to have their cake, and they want to eat it, too. Not me. I'm just going to sit and stare at it ... it's just so pretty.

Now, you know the type of people I do mind? Not the 98 percent that just want to have their cake and eat it, too. It's the ones who want to have *my* cake and they want to eat it, too—just for spite! Or how about the ones who devour their cake, and after finishing it, *still* want to have it, too. Isn't that the height of physics-defying greed?

Hey, how was that cake, man?

It was delicious ... I wolfed down the whole freakin' thing. And you know what? I still have it, too.

- **"Wow, you really know that** *("that"* could refer to something relevant, such as fifteenth-century Austrian botany) **like the back of your hand."**

Thank you, I think.

How well do *you* know the back of *your* hand? Me? I tend to get the fronts and backs of my hands confused. Why is the side that always shows called the back of my hand? I don't call the crabgrass in front of my house the *backyard.* And if I do find the back of my hand, what do I know about it other than it has four fingers plus a thumb, that a ring goes on one of the fingers, that the index finger picks my nose and other areas, and the middle finger is reserved for saluting other drivers?! Truth be told, if I know anything like the back of my hand, I don't know squat about it, and you should give me the finger just for thinking I'm an expert about it in the first place.

- *Matt, I know you just lost your job, your wife's ready to leave you, and you look like crap, but you know what ...* **Keep Your Chin Up!**

Wow, great advice there. Not only do I have no job, my marriage is on its last legs, and I look like warmed-over succotash, but I now have to go to a chiropractor three times a week for the rest of my life because I've been walking around with my chin pointing to the sky for the last month.

- *I haven't seen him in a* ***month of Sundays.*** You may want to use a new calendar there, pal.

- I'm not cleaning that toilet.

Just do it.

No, I won't.

Just do it, ***for Pete's sake!***

Heck, yeah!! You didn't tell me it was for Pete's sake. Just give me that cleanser and brush and let me have at it. Only for you, Pete.

So, what's the problem? First of all I don't even know who the heck Pete is, and he's motivating me to do odious things like cleaning toilets. All for his sake? I'm a big tennis fan, and I wouldn't clean someone else's toilet even for Pete Freakin' Sampras. Heck, I'm not doing it for anyone's sake ... for crying out loud. Oops, that's another idiot-matic expression: **FOR CRYING OUT LOUD!** Either shout out loud or don't; don't tell us that you're substituting another loud voice because it's somehow preferable to crying out loud. My baby cries out loud and it's effective and not all that unpleasant—once you get used to it. Have we forgotten that lesson?

- So, how did you like that movie?

It was ***the cat's pajamas!***

Huh?

Consider this scenario. Billy just had sex for the first time—with someone else. And the woman looks at him and says, "Well, how was I?" And Billy is so nervous that the only idiot-matic expression he can come up with is: "Wow, you were the cat's pajamas."

"Really?" she asks.

"Well, I exaggerated a little. Maybe more like the dog's nightgown."

Billy then gets kicked out of the room quite unceremoniously. Which was completely unfair because he just paid Blossom good money for their time together.

But maybe Billy deserved such treatment. I mean, who the heck thought that *the cat's pajamas* was a good thing to begin with, and who lodged that idiot-matic expression in his head? I've never seen a pajama-wearing cat, have you? Not even *The Cat in the Stinkin' Hat* wore PJs, and if he had worn them, would that have been a good thing? Would they be comfortable and stimulating enough for someone to use as a metaphor for, um, I don't know ... a minute and a half of mind-blowing paid sex?

- Here's one more for you:

*Matt, I'm sorry that I stole your new car, planted drugs in the glove compartment, and then crashed it into a brick wall. But hey, just **forgive and forget**. **Forgive and forget.***

For-what, and for-who?! Listen, jerkweed, I may in time forgive you if you do enough *'splaining*, buy me a new car, and get rid of the drugs, but you want me to forget what happened? What am I, a moron with no memory? (I urge you not to answer that.)

Of all the expressions, this may be the one that bothers me the most. I believe in forgiveness—it's a most powerful thing. I just don't believe that we should go around forgetting just so we can forgive. In fact, the best way to forgive is to remember, so that we don't screw up the next time around.

Forgive and forget. How stupid. Don't ever tell me that—for crying out loud! For Pete's sake! I don't want to hear that advice if I live for another whole year of freaking Sundays.

And, while you're at it, if I give you a cake, I expect you to eat it, too. I may even make you a delicious chocolate cake. You can even eat the whole darn thing with your chin down, for all I care.

2010

Palatable Oreo Hoagies

January 2010

Toastmasters International seems to encourage it and so do certain Hebrew school faculties, and both of these clubs—of which I am a member—reminded me of the benefits of the "Oreo Method" just this past week. And no, I wasn't licking up the creamy middle, or even drinking any milk at either meeting. Perhaps, just a little Kool-Aid.

As an officer of my Toastmasters club in Voorhees, New Jersey, I attended a Philadelphia district training session, where one of the presenters talked about the importance of using the Oreo Method when giving speech evaluations. It should be noted that the raison d'etre of Toastmasters is to give and evaluate speeches. So what is this method all about? Simply this. When critiquing a fellow member—even if his/her speech was of the lowest quality imaginable—one should always start with a positive, and end with a positive. Evidently, the middle doesn't have to be so, um, creamy.

For example, while I might otherwise wish to lambaste a fellow member for a horrific speech, I must do so in accordance with this principle. I may be thinking the following:

"John, I observed almost nothing of value in tonight's speech. You were nervous and uninspiring, and I had to slap myself awake at least thirteen times while you were rambling on as if you had three days to make your feeble points. By all means, please work on your preparation and your delivery before gracing our august podium again."

Utilizing the Oreo Method, I will now say: "John, you are to be commended for preparing and delivering your third speech this evening. There are some elements of delivery and time management that you are still learning to master. That being said, I await your fourth speech with bated breath, as do the members of our enthralled audience."

In the past week, I have learned that the Oreo Method is sometimes referred to as the Sandwich Method. Start with praise and end with praise; nobody will really remember the middle. I never knew that this technique had a name, but I am sure that I have employed a form of it in some of my past columns. If I reread some of these near-deadline rants, I will probably notice that the first and last paragraphs are pretty strong, but I won't necessarily vouch for the middles.

Growing up near Philadelphia, I should have realized the value of this approach. I have eaten many a sandwich, and certainly many a cheesesteak hoagie, where they could have, literally, put any old sh_t in the middle of it—the bread was that fresh and delicious. Around these parts, sandwiches and hoagies are truly all about the bread, as are, apparently, Hebrew school report cards at the synagogue where I teach on Saturday mornings.

At a very recent faculty meeting, our education director was going over the protocol for filling out report cards, which are to accentuate the positive, in keeping with best practices of the Oreo/Hoagie Method. So what happens when I'd like to point out that a certain student never does her homework, is rude, talks endlessly, and is quite disrespectful to her fellow students and her teacher each and every class? Simple: just prepare a nice little euphemism hoagie.

"Megan is to be commended for her fine attendance this semester. I envision that she will continue to encounter opportunities where she will be able to further master the art of channeling her energy in the most optimal ways. I look forward to seeing her progress in the coming term."

See that? Instead of making Megan or her parents feel lousy and risk a student dropping off our rolls, I just serve up a nice little crap hoagie, and even squeeze the crap out of the crap to render it less crappy. Even if this practice of weasel wording may strike me as distasteful, I have learned that with a little practice, a diluted crap hoagie is, I daresay, somewhat palatable.

Another important corroborating principle has just come to mind. Back in the day when I took a couple of psychology classes, I remember learning about primacy and recency effects. As I recall, a primacy effect occurs when you most remember the first item of a sequence, and a recency effect occurs when you most remember the last item. Almost all of the information that we assimilate comes from either the beginning or the end of a sequence. This reinforces my belief that when evaluating someone, you may say or write whatever you want in the middle, because the one being evaluated will only really remember the beginning or the end. I would speak more of primacy and recency, but I took these classes during college, where in a *good* semester, I attended the first and last classes. I never attended the middle classes—didn't have to.

All this has me thinking that I should use the Oreo Hoagie Method, even when not afraid of offending fellow Toastmasters or religious school parents and children. Just think of the following four scenarios, and how you might approach them with this wonderful technique.

Your softball teammate just lost a game for your team because of an utterly asinine baserunning gaffe. *Yo, Dave, you are a great guy, and a highly skilled lawyer. Having said that, you have absolutely no business doing anything even remotely quasi-athletic, as you just committed the single most boneheaded base-running mistake I have ever seen in my forty-five years of watching and playing baseball. Oh, I almost forgot: be sure to send my regards to Emma and your lovely children.*

Your husband forgot to take out the trash once again. *Honey, you are very accomplished in many important aspects of life, such as snoring, sports viewing, and belching. However, you are an ill-mannered sloth who never listens to me, and because of that, you have left our whole house smelling like your armpits before your all-too-infrequent showers. I look forward to your continued improvement in this area and hope that we will have occasion to spend the rest of our lives together.*

My neighbor's Doberman has just dropped yet another load of doo-doo on my lawn that he refuses to clean up. *Say, Tommy, your lawn is looking quite pristine these days. You may wish to contrast its appearance with that of mine, which has been soiled once again by that wretched, ugly, flatulent varmint that you call a house pet. While I would like to bestow a beating on your beloved Bowser, there may be a learning opportunity in store for its hideously overweight, lazy, inconsiderate owner. I look forward to your perfecting the scoop technique, and I look forward to our next block party.*

Breaking up with your girlfriend. (If *boyfriend* is apropos, just change the type of meat in the middle.) *Edna, you have been a faithful companion these past five months, and I appreciate your many displays of loyalty. However, I have observed that there are opportunities for you to master the concepts of faithfulness, social etiquette, appearance, intelligent discourse, and overall humanity. I feel that you can best perfect these few areas without me as an impediment, and I wish you every happiness in pursuing all of your dreams and ambitions.*

You may have noticed that these sample Oreo Hoagies differed in their bread-to-meat ratios. Not to worry. This is as much art as it is science, and you will soon discover various ways to prepare such sandwiches. Some scenarios will almost cry out for a lot of stuffing, and others will call for comparatively skimpy fillings. You be the judge. But by all means, please make sure that your breading is of the very highest quality.

Heaters to Hawaiians

February 2010

I won't lie to you. There are many things in life that have always frustrated me, but looking for work has to be the most singularly frustrating of them all. In all my adult years, I have never embarked upon a very effective career search, and I resent that I find myself right now in the position of having to do so again. Perhaps, if I ever learned how to do it well, I would: 1) not have to do it now, or 2) not mind doing it again, even in this economy.

So, where does an open-minded type with a somewhat mercurial psyche look for work? Or better yet, what does he look for? Well, not knowing how to pigeonhole myself, and not really knowing how to explain (excuse?) my résumé, I usually end up looking for something in sales. Truth be told, when I do land interviews, I handle them fairly well. When the time comes, I project confidence and feign enough interest, and I am a somewhat articulate *sonofagun*. So what's the problem? Well, I won't lie to you: I have a somewhat mercurial psyche. If you're scoring at home, that's *two* problems right there.

In the last year, my mediocre job search has led me to interview for two financial services companies. In both cases, I hit it off well with the interviewer prior to being forced to take one of those career profile tests. These state-of-the-industry diagnostic tests are supposedly designed to test your aptitude for sales and entrepreneurship, and they certainly test your ability and patience to navigate a minefield of insipid, nonsensical inquiries.

For each multiple-choice question, I tried my best to hold my nose and pick the letter that corresponded to the answer that least offended or befuddled me. I restrained myself from screaming, "This is bullsh_t," but I still found myself unable or unwilling to attain a score that would earn another interview. I never found out the exact result of either test, but my score on the second one—which I took online—inspired this response from the recruiter, an acne-faced dude who I remember as Skippy Dumasky. (To be fair, I am paraphrasing both his name and his e-mail):

Tsk. Tsk. You did not meet our company's cutoff score on our career profile screening. This means that your likelihood of succeeding in a financial services sales career is statistically lower than my chance of marrying Megan Fox. Your rating indicates that other people like you who were contracted as financial sales representatives failed to produce in the top half of the company, and either committed suicide or enrolled in the witness protection program. At this time I would suggest you consider a different career choice, such as cow tipping or humor writing. If you are still alive one year from now, please contact me.

Well, at least Skippy (who, come to think of it, had the charisma of a rice cake), did not rule out my reapplying to his company, and he did generously suggest a career alternative or two.

With those suggestions in mind, I recently checked some ads online. (Did you know that besides offering everything from used furniture to full body massage, Craigslist also has a jobs board?) So, of course, I went right to the sales/biz development section and soon found an ad trumpeting that their position would offer unlimited income potential and the opportunity to be my own boss. Wow! Although I had never heard of Igloonatic Marketing before, I had to admit that the name sounded kind of cool. I was able to set up an interview with a garrulous sort named Harvey Blandings. Our conversation went like this.

Harvey: So Matt, I'm looking at your résumé, and it's very impressive in a descriptive kind of way.

Matt: Why, thank you, Mr. Blandings. (I still don't know why I threw in the "why" before the "thank you.")

Harvey: It's Harvey. Call me Harve. Let me jump right to the shark here. Can you sell ice to an Eskimo?

Matt: Excuse me, Harve. But that's kind of a cliché, isn't it? But yes, on my best days, I think I can. (Okay, I can lie to an interviewer, but never to a client or friend.)

Harvey: Well, do you have a lot of "best days"?

Matt: Sure. On a good week, I have at least four or five of them, with at least three coming on weekdays.

Harvey: Terrific. Igloonatic sales reps have a lot of good days. So tell me, are you self-motivated?

Matt: Absolutely, seeing as nobody else is able to motivate me, I would conclude so.

Harvey: Do you like being your own boss?

Matt: On a good week, I do. Yet, quite frankly, there are times where I do enjoy being browbeaten and generally bossed around by others.

Harvey: Hmm, I see. Well tell me again, can you sell ice to an Eskimo?

Matt: Is it necessary to be able to sell ice to an Eskimo?

Harvey: Well, we at Igloonatic seem to think it is. Our company was founded in 1967, and in the last forty-two-plus years, we have sold millions of blocks of ice and ice cream products to Eskimos.

Matt: I did not realize that. Why don't you sell them heaters or gloves or thermal underwear? I think I could do that if the prices are competitive.

Harvey: That's not what we do. No challenge in that. So do you think you have what it takes to sell ice to Eskimos?

Matt: Now that you've challenged part of my manhood, I think I can embrace that challenge.

Harvey: Great, because I need someone like you with a resolute psyche to sell to the Inuits and the Yup'iks of western Alaska. Wonderful people, really. We have a brand new, protected territory with unlimited income potential, and all of our sales brochures are provided at no cost to our reps.

Matt: No cost. Hmmm. So do I get reimbursed for my phone calls?

Harvey: Phone calls? We don't do telemarketing. At Igloonatic, we go right to people's homes. Would you be able to relocate?

Matt: Well, I'd need to run it by my wife first. I'm sure you would pick up the cost of relocating.

Harvey: Here's what we do. Keep all of your receipts related to moving costs, and I mean everything. If after the first year you finish in the top half of our sales team, I will reimburse you in full.

Matt: Oh, okay, I could do that. How many sales reps do you have?

Harvey: Right now, it's just me. And you should be able to outsell an old windbag like me, right?

Matt: I'm not sure how to answer that, Harve. Can you tell me about Igloonatic's benefits?

Harvey: First of all, you get all the benefits of being your own boss. You set your own hours and work outside in the fresh air with a minimum of paperwork. Secondly, did I mention that you have an uncapped earnings potential? As far as health care, we don't exclude you from getting any type of health insurance you may want for yourself and your family. We just don't believe that we should have to pay for it. Does that make sense?

Matt: Yes, about as much sense as selling ice cream to an Eskimo, I guess.

Harvey: Exactly. So when would you like to start?

Matt: Well, assuming my wife goes for it, and I tidy up some loose ends here, and check out the school districts of coastal Alaska, can you give me about a month?

Harve: Ya got it.

Matt: Oh, Harve, I do have a question for you.

Harvey: Sure, what do ya got?

Matt: Do you have a division of Igloonatic that sells, say, heaters to Hawaiians, or pineapples to Polynesians, or ...

Harvey: No, we don't. But, that's something to consider when we expand. I'll tell you what, Matt. I appreciate your time, and I hope you'll consider our generous offer and get back to me within one week. Now, is what I see on your résumé your correct e-mail address?

Matt: Sure is.

Harvey: Great. I'm going to pass along just a little more info about my company. And then, I need a half hour of your time to take a little test. We call it the ICE test, which stands for Igloonatic Career Evaluation. It's an ingenious little multiple choice diagnostic tool that evaluates who can really sell. You don't have a problem taking a little test like that do you, Matt?

Matt: No, not at all.

Harvey: Terrific. So, after you pass our test, I'll call you to set up the next interview. I'll see you soon.

Matt: I wouldn't be so sure of that, Harve.

News Flash: Anatomy of a Column

March 2010

Watching the 11:00 pm local news usually both interests and confounds me somewhat, and my experience a few nights ago was no different from the usual. To be accurate, the newscast followed late-night coverage of the Vancouver Winter Olympics, and I was just waking up from an ice dance–inspired nap, when I saw the urgent report of suburban Philly police apprehending a suspect whom they believed to be the Perkiomen Trail Flasher.

I'm not so sure if this was the top story of the day, and I really hadn't been following this story or the local news at all of late. (At 11:00 pm, I'd much rather be doing something more valuable, like helping to get my now nineteen-month-old Benny to bed or watching *Seinfeld* reruns.) I had not even heard of the PT Flasher, even if my new abbreviation makes him sound like the semireliable Chrysler that I sometimes drive. And maybe I figured that a flasher who plied his trade forty or so miles away from my home/workplace was of no great concern to me.

The report, however, did get my attention, and I was more than half awake when I saw the local cops lead a burly white guy to a van. In a scene that struck me as ironic, the notorious PT Flasher was trying everything in his power to cover up his face, even as the cameras kept finding new angles to, um, expose him.

I was able to sleep in about fifteen minutes' time and woke up again a few hours later with a few thoughts—however well baked—in mind:

- Who was this guy, and what did he allegedly do and to whom?
- Why was this deemed an important story?
- Why would someone be equally dedicated to both (allegedly) exposing his manhood and covering up his face-hood?
- Is any of this fodder for a future column?

Not knowing what to write about, I answered the last question in the affirmative, and like the local TV camera people, started exploring new angles for this column.

Who Was/Is This Guy and What Did He Do?

I thought I would try to shed some light on, prior to making light of, this story. Doing a quick search online, I found a story from a couple weeks back, which I am *borrowing:*

Per state police at the Skippack (PA) barracks, a forty-seven-year-old woman and a fifty-year-old woman were out for a walk on the portion of the trail near the intersection of Gravel Pike and Plank Road around 4:08 PM. A man dressed in dark sweatpants and a light-colored, hooded sweatshirt started walking behind them, the women told police. When the two women turned around, they saw the man pull what looked like a ski mask over his face before he put his hands into his pants, police said. He then pulled down his pants and exposed his genitals to the women, police said.

I am still not sure if this guy had exhibited himself to anyone other than these two unfortunate women and I am truly happy that this creep apparently did not threaten these women in any other way.

Unanswered Questions

- Why a ski mask? Even though I've been watching a lot of these Olympics events, I wonder if skiers still wear ski masks, or simply cool helmets? Are ski masks still the *facegear* of choice for bank robbers and flashers?
- Why did he pick the intersection of Gravel and Plank? Was this an accidental destination, or is there some kind of weird symbolism there that I can't/won't spell out?
- Assuming any thought goes into something so thoughtless and idiotic, why did the PT Flasher decide to pull it out on a cold winter day?

Why Was This Deemed Newsworthy?

Obviously, PT Flasher himself should have been covered, but why was this story covered? Was it a slow news day? I missed the first part of the newscast, but it may well have opened like this:

Bode Miller skis for gold, and President Obama is retooling his health care reform package, but the big story on Action News is the apparent apprehension by Perkiomen Township police of a man who illegally showed his retooled package to two horrified women who were out for a walk on a nature trail. The so-called Perkiomen Trail Flasher ...

Greater minds than mine, and hopefully there are some, may debate whether this story was newsworthy. Perhaps I shouldn't make light of that aspect. I would be up in arms if my wife were exposed to Mr. Flash, and would be mortified if my baby—even a slightly older version of him—were similarly exposed. In fact, I have decidedly mixed feelings every time Baby Ben pushes open our bathroom door when I am enthroned, or standing up to heed nature's call. I don't want to put locks on any of our doors and am not all that comfortable with him seeing me in this state, even if my wife and I regularly, and necessarily, see him this way. I am thankful that I have no such memories of spying on my own dad, and I hope that Benny's memories won't really kick in until such a point when I can yell at him to "stay out" and he'll obey me.

Otherwise, I can just imagine the type of free-wheeling conversations he may have with his friends in high school or college: "Yeah, dude, I used to barge in on my dad also, and it was really gross. He had lousy aim, and when he stood up, it was ... " I've admittedly taken some liberties here; I'm not sure if "dude" and "gross" will still be in vogue fifteen or so years from now.

Still Unanswered Questions

- Should this story have made the news at all?
- Was there a sense of relief when he was apprehended?
- Was the original story, including the nickname "Perkiomen Trail Flasher" *all hat, and no cattle*?

The Mentality of the Flasher

Doing light research is so easy nowadays, and while it's tricky to rely on "wiki," I did a search for "flashing" on Wikipedia.org, and found the information to be both of interest and plausible enough. Flashing, I learned, is just one of many types of exhibitionism. There is "mooning," but usually showing one's derriere in public is laughed off as a prank, and even Action News would probably not cover stories of a PT Mooner. Well, maybe they would, but...

There's also the female flasher, but my opinion is that a woman who flashes her breasts (and I hold this firmly) is not considered to be a nuisance nor a potential predator like the male flasher. And if she does flash her breasts for beads, she enters whole new categories: a hero to the morons who watch Jerry Springer, and an idol to millions of Mardi Gras celebrants.

Per Wikipedia, there's also something known as apodysophilia, or the "Lady Godiva Syndrome," which sounds one heck of a lot more interesting than a burly guy with a ski mask and a major problem in the middle of a nature trail. But back to our everyday garden-variety flasher: A group of 185 exhibitionists was asked, "How would you have preferred a person to react if you were to expose your privates to him or her?" The results were as follows:

- Would want to have sexual intercourse—35.1%
- No reaction necessary at all—19.5%
- Would want them to show their privates also—15.1%
- Admiration—14.1%
- Any reaction—11.9%
- Anger and disgust—3.8%
- Fear—0.5%

Looking at the survey—and I never heard this question asked on *The Family Feud*—I am not sure what to make of it. The first reply is somewhat troubling, and validates the concern that flashing should not be laughed off, even if it may not be front-page news material. But if you take away the first and third replies, the others are quite normal, even if they are reactions to an abnormal activity/compulsion/problem.

In fact, if humor columnists, standup comedians, artists, and beach volleyball players alike were queried on how they would want a person to react to their *exhibitions*, perhaps there would be a similar mix of: no reaction (needed), admiration, any reaction (at all), anger, disgust, and fear. And, perhaps, "sexual intercourse" and "wanting others to show their stuff" would also find their way on our lists, if we were being frank. Hmmm ...

Still Unanswered Questions

So now that we know just a little bit more about the mentality of someone like the PT Flasher, do we still have to ask:

- Why would someone so eager to expose himself be so concerned with covering his face?
- Was he just showing off his new ski mask?

Fodder for Future Columns

Okay, even if I didn't shed any great light here or produce anything of great weight, I am satisfied enough with my exploration to call this a *column*, "Tip of the Goldberg"-style.

Still Unanswered Questions

- Will this accidental news flash and new column (perhaps newsworthy to only me) inspire future columns?
- Will these future columns be *better,* and who exactly judges such things?
- Will I continue my quest for the perfect column, and what thoughts—dark, light, and otherwise—will I expose myself and my readers to?

Please stay tuned, and thank you for reading with (only) an open mind.

Ignoring Our Please

April 2010

There are millions of beautiful babies out there in the U.S. alone, and most self-respecting, loving parents out there think that they have the most perfect one. I won't argue with any of them—since I *am* one of them—yet I know that I am the father of the most perfect baby on the planet. I speak, of course, of the now twenty-month-old Baby Ben ...

Please allow me a digression: When do we stop counting the age of human beings in months? I know I stopped doing it for myself a long time ago, which I think is a good thing. It relieves me of the burden of trying to figure out how to use my cell phone calculator and hearing people say things like, "Wow, you look great for six hundred months. I thought you were only four hundred ninety or so." My guess is that we'll stop counting months for *Baby Ben* (and, I guess he'll have to lose *that* moniker as well) at about twenty-four. Which is also a good thing, as twenty-five will exceed the sum of my fingers, toes, eyes, and ears.

... Now, back to my boasting. Please don't take the first paragraph to mean that Baby Ben is perfect; he's just the most perfect baby I know of, and he's absolutely perfect for us. And if the price of having an absolutely perfect baby is living with his apparent imperfections, this seems like a ridiculously small price to pay for all of the indescribable joy that he gives us most of his loving, creative, silly, perplexing, and unique moments. So what if he refuses to let us put him into his crib before midnight, or if he raises a big fuss (about the only time he ever cries) when we shut off the TV. That's no big deal—right? Is it? The wife and I are still debating this one.

A friend of mine who is a fellow sports lover has not had the pleasure of meeting Baby Ben as yet. He asked me by e-mail if BB had attained any milestones of late, and I wasn't sure how to answer him. When you observe someone so closely, you run the risk of counting every raised eyebrow as a milestone, but you may also miss some of the big stuff. The only thing that made sense to my way of thinking was to give him a scouting report, in the manner that a baseball bird dog may write to his employer about a certain young (but still more than two hundred months, in most cases) prospect.

Benjamin Jun Goldberg
Date Observed: Afternoon of March 23, 2010
Date of Birth: July 24, 2008
Height: I forget
Weight: 25.5 pounds

Observations: *Runs around pretty well and shows good acceleration, especially when being chased ... teaching himself how to jump ... exhibits a powerful throwing arm for his age, if not overly accurate or too discriminating about what he throws or who he throws to/at ... shows physical toughness in bouncing back after falls, with minimal if any crying ... good team player, good hugger—but has not given too many high-fives of late ...*

great stage presence and charisma with a contagious laugh and smile ... building an unofficial vocabulary of about seventy words and expressions, the majority in Mandarin ... displaying an addiction to TV (and loves to watch and say "hockey") ... will pick up books and start to act out parts ... loves the playground, and he is starting to enjoy slides as much as swings ... plays well with others.

Conclusion: *While a little bit of a free spirit, his intelligence, humor, playfulness, and cuteness is off the charts. Still time to be a great point guard, tennis player, slick middle infielder, or scatback—or maybe a nifty right winger. Nobel Peace Prize and Pulitzer are definite possibilities if he shows more determination and resolve than his old man ever did.*

While our prodigy is still very much in the running for a professional sports career, literary immortality, musical greatness, Jewish-style sainthood, and so much more, I'm realistic enough to know that there are obstacles he will encounter the next ten thousand months or so along the way. Some of the obstacles are provided by a kiddie play/school place in a neighboring township. Ruby and I drive him to Little Sport and, given his youth, attend class with him.

If this serves as a plug for Little Sport (they're in Maple Shade, New Jersey, by the way), so be it; we really enjoy the place, and the owner and all of the instructors (called *coaches*) are very fine people. The forty-five-minute or so rookies class is led by a young lady named Coach Kaitlin, who leads parents and little ones through a combination of structured exercises, little sing-songs (as opposed, I guess, to songs that you don't sing), light introductions to sports, obstacle courses, parent-guided play, balloons, parachutes, and bubbles. If this sounds like an action-packed forty-five minutes, it is; good thing, as it's about the only workout I get most weeks.

So what's the problem? I love everything about this class but the obstacle course. Only it's not the obstacle course itself, but the prelude to the obstacle course that provides the biggest obstacle to my enjoying this class completely. About fifteen minutes into the class, Coach Kaitlin calls the kids over to home plate whereupon the babies—some more quickly than others—amble over and tap the plate a few times. At this point, Benny's usually in the middle of the pack. So far, okay. Then the shtick is that the kids have to either say or sign "please." The reward for doing so is the chance to hold a beanbag (of the color of the day) while they traipse around the course.

Let me set the usual scene for you. Coach holds up a little beanbag, and Lauren and Dominic immediately both say and sign "please." Another one or two of the gang of six manage to act beanbag-worthy, which leaves Benny and maybe one other baby holding the—er, not holding the bag. A month or so ago, Ruby or I could signal for him, but we're not allowed to do that anymore. Coach Kaitlin, while young, wasn't born yesterday and she wants to instill graciousness and good manners in her little charges. Perhaps while I'm a few feet away praying to the beanbag gods, another little one will have said or signed the magic word, and now all eyes appear to be on my boy, who admittedly, everyone in the room is still hopelessly in love with, but ...

... Daddy can't bear to watch as Benny keeps holding his hand out and expecting a beanbag to magically be placed on top of it. Or maybe he knows he won't get it but is testing her resolve. Or maybe ... I'm not sure what to think. With rare exception, seeing and hearing no evidence of "please" from Baby Ben, Coach will hand us the beanbag, and leave it to our discretion as to whether Benny gets to lug one around the obstacle course. At this point, the music plays and Benny joins the line of babies and parents stepping, crawling, sliding, and rolling their way around the bases. When he's not exploring the outfield or other areas of the Little Sport arena/classroom, BB does a great job with his movement—exhibiting grace and coordination that his dad probably did not display till at least thirty months or so.

So what of Baby Benny's Beanbag Boycott? Ruby does not think it's a big deal, allowing that Benny is so young and still one of the two youngest babies in the class. He cooperates well in most of the other parts of the class and is one of the better cleaner-uppers. She also takes this as an opportunity to remind me of my penchant for overanalysis and worrying too much about things—most things besides earning a practical living, I (or she) might add.

My take? I have considered all of the following theories and ramifications and then some, including:

- What if Benny does not know how to make the sign for *please* or say the word with some degree of accuracy? No, this can't be the case, as he's done a couple of other signs, and has said much tougher words.
- What if Benny doesn't like Coach? Nah—she's very nice, and there's no carryover to other parts of the class. Besides, he's never mentioned anything.
- What if he just needs a breather, and is taking a rest before the obstacle course? This seems to have some degree of merit,

but no—he seems to be blessed with great energy.

- What if he just wants to embarrass Daddy (and to a lesser extent Mommy) for some reason—he must have an arsenal of reasons by now. Can't be the case, can it? He's too young for that type of thinking. Isn't he?
- Okay, what if he never ever says *please* in the future? Maybe he dislikes the word, and realizes that Mommy and Daddy get whatever they want around the house—well, within reason—without ever having to sign or say it. And at home, a simple cry (usually a quick crocodile cry) will usually get him the toy or TV time that he needs. Are we creating a monster here? Albeit, a beautiful, sweet, brilliant, will-never-hurt-anyone type of monster … I'm not sure.

Of course, there may be another explanation that I have been loath to consider. Benny is not a big fan of beanbags, at least not the type that one holds in one's hands. When he visited my brother in Israel one year ago, he did enjoy sitting on a beanbag chair, and I even called him "Bean Bag Benny" once or twice. But sitting on a huge beanbag and carrying a little beanbag are two completely different activities. I have also noticed that even on the rare occasion that Benny *earns* his Little Sport beanbag, he often discards it intentionally. And when he does so inadvertently, he does not seem too upset when he leaves it in the middle of one of the tunnels that he just crawled through. Perhaps, this new theory is gaining some traction with me. So if this is the case, what does all this mean? The wheels turn.

Will Benny be the type of boy and man that won't have exceptional manners? It's possible but way too early to tell. Will he grow up not loving beanbags? If so, no great tragedy there. Will he be disrespectful to authority figures—like coaches, rabbis, and teachers? Nothing else seems to point to that. Will Benny be willing to go against the grain, and not feel that he has to have something he doesn't like (or need) just to be one of the gang? Probably, and is that such a bad thing? Of course not.

As I'm up at 2 am pondering such things, I wonder how my little guy's personality will develop over the years. Will he be the quiet observer type, as he appeared to be during his first twelve months? Probably not, as he's been jabbering away at a pretty good pace ever since. Will he be given to introspection, as his dad surely is? Yes, but I don't think that he will inherit all the ways I manage to tie myself into knots of indecision, making simple tasks my own personal obstacle courses.

It's quite natural, I suppose, for all parents to wonder about such things, even if not all (or very many) of them would attach so much significance to this beanbag mystery. I rationalize that all this effort is worth it, as I am continually fascinated by this little guy and I love him so completely that I find myself both laughing and crying as I try to coax the proper words from my clumsy fingers. I will be so proud of him when he emulates what I feel are my better qualities, and my heart will break each time when I fear that he will exhibit my lesser ones. Maybe, he will figure all this stuff out better than I ever did or will—just as I suppose that he may have already solved this beanbag dilemma that so perplexes me.

As I write, Benny and Ruby are in New York for a week, spending time with her family—mostly to be with Benny's grandma, who underwent a medical procedure today. I am gratified that Benny already seems to have great love and appreciation for his two living grandparents, the aforementioned grandma, known as "Waipaw," and my own dad, whom he greets joyfully with the Mandarin "Yei-Yei." I am happy that he is with her, but the insecure, jealous (lesser?) side of me is missing him very much.

I won't get to play with him in person for almost eight days, and I have nobody to read to, or throw a silly ball with, or share any number of amazing things with that don't necessarily show up as milestones. There are certain smiles and bits of shared laughter that can't be quantified on scouting reports, and having turned off some YouTube videos, I am almost haunted by how quiet and boring it is right now.

One day, Benny will read this (not sure if that pleases or scares me more), and I hope that he will recognize a great measure of the deep love I have for him. I am sure that his amazing smile and laugh—so heartwarming that strangers as well as people we know just have to stop what they're doing to steal a moment or two with him—will always be present, whether he is twenty months old or eight hundred.

Going forward, I hope and pray that his sense of joy and wonder will never diminish, or be overtaken by pessimism, self-doubt, laziness, or cynicism. I hope that I will have the strength of faith to remind him—should he ever need it—that the world, despite its many imperfections, is a great place, and that he is one of the people that will make it even greater, and kinder, and more joyous.

Indeed, I will also counsel my lesser instincts to not demand perfection from him as I or others may seek to define it. Because after all, he is the most perfect human being I have ever laid eyes on and opened my heart to, and I hope that all parents feel that way about their children. And yes, it would be nice if many children felt that way about their parents—even after they have been on this planet for more than twenty months.

All this introspection and near-maudlin sentimentality—did I cross that line yet?—has me wanting to revisit that most imperfect scouting report of mine.

Benjamin Jun Goldberg
Date Observed: Early morning of March 24, 2010
Date of Birth: same as before
Height: I still forget
Weight: 25.5 pounds, and growing

Observations: A mysterious, infectious ball of energy, joy, and bewilderment ... shows a strange aversion to beanbags and/or saying/signing the word "please" ... finds joy in almost everything, with the above being one of very few exceptions to that rule ... seems to value happiness over conformity, but that is a projection on my part ... can be quite mischievous ... finds humor in almost everything ... loves his family, but says *Mama* seven times for every *Da-da*—not that I'm counting or anything ...

Conclusion: His potential is without any known limit ... he will find and choose the path that works for him ... who knows: he may even win the Nobel *Please* Prize.

Sports Shrinkage

May 2010

In an effort to understand and possibly cure my addiction to watching and thinking about sports, I made an appointment to see psychologist Dr. Marta Hari, a featured character in my upcoming *Wordapodia* book—and the author of the seminal scholarly work *Young Head Cases*. After the typical greetings, the conversation unfolded like this:

Marta: So Matt, you said that you're worried about all the time you waste watching sports, and also ruminating about sports. I suspect that you also have a problem with betting on sports. Is that true?

Matt: Not at all. I may eat, drink, sleep, and ruminate about sports, but I never bet on them. I'm too broke.

Marta: Well, that's good—in a sense. But that's also a little like the husband boasting, *I may cheat on my wife, but it's not like I've forced myself on anyone.* Or, the defendant saying, *I may have held up several banks, but I've never fired my gun at anyone.* Or—

Matt: I get it. But I'm paying good money for your time and expertise, and hope you can focus on my addiction with as few analogies as possible.

Marta: Analogies work because they illustrate a point. You should consider my "No Excuses" group therapy sessions on Tuesday evenings. They're very therapeutic.

Matt: That's interesting. You mean you devote a whole series of sessions to getting people out of their habit of excuse making?

Marta: It started out that way. But now, we mostly exchange various excuses that we have used over the years. Kind of like how a cooking class exchanges recipes.

Matt: You charge people a lot of money to master the art of excuse making? Aren't you exploiting your clientele?

Marta: That's a gross oversimplification on your part. I might charge my clients and not help them break their habits, but it's not as if any of my clients complain—or go bankrupt.

Matt: Good example, Doc.

Marta: Let's get back to the issue at hand. How long have you been incurably addicted to sports?

Matt: Well, I think I got hooked on baseball at about age seven, and the other sports followed shortly thereafter.

Marta: I see. That's a whole bunch of years. Do you think that one session is going to cure you?

Matt: No, I never said that. And, it hasn't been *that* long.

Marta: I think you may be in denial.

Matt: Denial?! I was the one who contacted your office for this appointment.

Marta: I know that. I think you're in denial about your age. Tell me: Which sports do you seem to be addicted to watching and thinking about?

Matt: There's major league baseball and pro football, basketball, and hockey. College football and basketball, tennis and golf, and I'm glued to the Olympics when they come on. That's about it.

Marta: Okay, let's call it eight sports times forty or so years. That's three hundred twenty or so addiction points. How about NASCAR? Or boxing? Or bowling? Or wrestling?

Matt: Not really, seldom, no, and no. Although now that Danica Patrick is in NASCAR, I'm inclined to tune in from time to time.

Marta: Why, exactly? So you could see her Go Daddy–sponsored car drive into the pit stop and then come in last place?

Matt: She's had some good results, even if no top tens on the Nationwide series this year, but you want to know why I watch?

Marta: I'm paid to listen.

Matt: I love it when she gets out of the car, and shakes her long black hair out of her helmet. Very sexy.

Marta: Noted: helmet hair fetishist. Did you also tell me that you're a Philadelphia sports fan?

Matt: Absolutely. I root hard for all the Philly teams, unless they trade away my favorite players. When that happens, I try to root for the Philly team, but my loyalty to my favorite ex-player also kicks in and I root for that team as well. Case in point: did you know that my Eagles just traded Donovan McNabb?

Marta: Of course. So what? He was there for eleven years and never won the Super Bowl.

Matt: He was our best player and got us close all those years. He's a Hall of Fame quarterback, and I hope he beats the Eagles and wins a Super Bowl with the Redskins. It wasn't his fault we didn't win the Super Bowl. He won a ton of games for us.

Marta: Excuses, excuses. So, let's recap. Forty years of addiction times eight sports, throw in your Danica Patrick hair fetish and the fact that you're a Philly sports fan with divided loyalty syndrome. Let's see: five hundred-plus addiction points. I would recommend one hour of treatment every week for the next ten years, and then we'll reassess. Tell me: How do you waste time thinking about sports when you're not watching sports?

Matt: I listen to the idiots on sports talk radio. I read the sports section online and get into sports chats and arguments. I talk about sports with my friends. I make lists of favorite players and who I think should make the Hall of Fame in their respective sports. That's about it.

Marta: What does your lovely wife think about all this, um, commitment to sports on your part?

Matt: Well, she doesn't know about the Hall of Fame lists, but she seems to be resigned to all this.

Marta: Poor lady. And how about the players that you get obsessed with? Do they spend their valuable time worrying about you?

Matt: That's an unfair question. They don't really know I exist.

Marta: Precisely. Do you remember that line from *A Bronx Tale?* The gangster Sonny is mentoring Calogero and tells him, "Mickey Mantle don't give a cr_p about you. He don't pay your rent." Ever see that film?

Matt: Good movie—just saw it for the first time last year and I agree. But I was already addicted to sports and my favorite players for a lot of years before I saw it. It's a good line, though.

Marta: Let's draw on this. You worry about which players—some of whom make at least ten million dollars a year—will get traded, and which ones will make the all-star team (and earn more bonus money) and which might make the Hall of Fame. If your football team—if you can figure out who to root for this coming year—loses on Sunday, you'll have a miserable week. If you tune in to NASCAR, or is it Nationwide, and Danica does not take her helmet off and toss her luscious hair, you get slightly depressed. Is all this true?

Matt: Essentially.

Marta: So do you spend one tenth of your sports time thinking about world hunger, the environment, your son's college fund, your overall finances, or world peace?

Matt: No, not really.

Marta: Do you want to really get outraged about something? Think about this: The great Meryl Streep has not won an Academy Award since 1983 for *Sophie's Choice*. She has been nominated twelve times since then—eleven as lead actress—and has walked away without the statuette each and every time. How about that?

Matt: That's remarkable, but does Meryl Streep care about you and pay your rent?

Marta: Meryl is a great lady and a superior actress who has great empathy and sympathy for everybody. And you wanna know a little secret? Ms. Streep is a client of mine. She sessions with me every year right before and after the Oscars.

Matt: Amazing. I'm not sure what to say.

Marta: Say you'll be here next week at the same time to start your second of about five hundred sessions together. I'll get to the root causes of this; I always do eventually.

Matt: Sounds good. Oh, may I ask a favor? I just remembered something. I need to change my appointment time next week. The Phillies are playing the Cardinals, and I'm a huge Albert Pujols fan.

Marta: That's okay. I knew you would say that. If you move your appointment to another day, I can sit home and watch the entire Joan Crawford film festival on TCM.

Afterword

September 2010

How many times have you heard the following cliché? *Everything happens for a reason.* I've heard this saying enough that I wish I had a dollar for every time someone has said it to me. Heck, I'm so broke that I wish I had a dollar for every time I've heard someone say, "Kocham grających tenisa podczas trzęsienia ziemi."

But seriously, I reject the notion that everything happens for a reason. I would change that truism to say that as (supposedly) intelligent beings we possess the power to assign reason to that which has happened. Not quite as catchy, but it rings truer to me.

My belief is that humorists, especially, try to assign reason to things that just don't make sense—these things could refer to anything within the strange worlds of sports, politics, business, entertainment and of course, family life.

In looking back at these columns that spin a narrative of sorts of the last almost three years of my life, I hope that I have made some sense of this part of my journey, and enabled you to relate to my life (or at least my mind) even if the circumstances of my life and my own beliefs may be quite different from yours.

Another belief that I cling to is that a humorist, at *his* core, is a very serious person; he is just blessed, and sometimes cursed, with a hyperactive sense of humor. Maybe I should not generalize this, but I know that this is true in my case.

When I started writing these columns, I was embarking on a slightly different type of writing for me—humorous essays—and I was not sure what to expect. I thought that I could get by with a satiric voice, and that tone still finds its way into my writing at times. I also found myself writing about more serious topics along the way, with the hope that these pieces were still entertaining, or at least resonant.

So, have I found reason in the strange behavior exhibited by institutions, family members, friends, and (um) me? Have I just shrugged my shoulders and pointed out some curiosities without any solution in mind? Yes, and yes.

Though unplanned, as I mostly wrote in real time as events or thoughts unfolded, one of the dominant themes of this book is my coming to grips with being a father—and doing so well into my forties. Do I have any regrets in this regard? Perhaps so, but let me qualify this apparent regret.

I very much wish that I would have been a father earlier in life—for scores of reasons. My own mom never got to meet Benny (and vice versa) and Ruby's dad also never got that opportunity.

More superficially, I worry about being young enough and energetic enough for my son as he gets older—I can fake it pretty well now—and while it would be cool if Benny adopts my love for sports, I don't want him kicking my butt at those sports before he turns ten or so.

These are regrets that I can't wire myself to push aside; self-forgiveness does not come easily to this hyperactive humorist. But let me also offer this counterpoint: I would not have wanted to be a father earlier in life if that would have changed anything about my son.

I stand by what I wrote about Benny in my April, 2010 column: "...I know that I am the father of the most perfect baby on the planet." And no, I don't intend to be one of those parents who can't or won't be able to see any imperfections in their little darlings. I just acknowledge that—imperfections and all—that I would not want to change anything about a little boy that I can't even think about without smiling, laughing and crying all at once.

So yes, if being a father earlier in life would have meant that Benny—as I now regard him—would be any less *Benny-like*, I would not have done so. Does this mean that everything in life happens for a reason? No, I also stand by my twist on this statement.

This book is close to going live, even if the columns of the last few months do not appear in this edition. It had to end somewhere, although my columns have continued and presumably will for a little while longer.

If there is a beauty to this book, it lies in its unscripted nature, if not in its writing. I'm not sure what the next three years will bring but I'm sure that I'll still be fascinated, thrilled and frightened by marriage and fatherhood, somewhat contemptuous of modern politics, journalism and the business world, and ever trying to make sense—in "Tip of the Goldberg-style—of all these oddities.

The more things change, the more they stay the same? Now that's a saying that I can more easily adopt.

Most of all, I want to once again thank my family for implicitly allowing me to write about them; this was not easy as we are essentially very private people. And I also want to thank you for reading this book and finding something of value that enabled you to read it and recommend it to others as well. Hopefully.

One last thought, or is it an afterthought? While I have left many loose ends in my life's narrative, I do not like to leave any loose ends in my writing. You may be wondering what *Kocham grających tenisa podczas trzęsienia ziemi* means.

Thanks to a Web site called www.worldlingo.com, I'm happy to report that this is Polish for *I love playing tennis during earthquakes.*

It may still be true that *All That Twitters is not Goldberg,* but I can't live without the internet—and I can't seem to write without the white noise of music and sports droning in the background.

About the Author

Matthew J. Goldberg is a uniquely dynamic writer and speaker noted for his irreverent, offbeat sense of humor. He is the author of the unintended cult classics, So So Wisdom and Mixed Emotions, as well as the just released ***Wordapodia, Volume One: An Encyclopedia of Real Fake Words***. All That Twitters Is Not Goldberg is a compendium of Matt's *The Tip of the Goldberg* humor columns—written as a monthly column for a writers' e-zine.

An accomplished, award-winning public speaker, Matt finds truthful humor in just about everything, including his late foray into fatherhood and trying to raise the perfect American Chinese Jewish baby, his addiction to sports (and the singular frustration of being a Philadelphia sports fan) and the hypocrisy of so many in the business world, in political life and within our media. Although real life provides plenty of material, he is not immune to flights of fancy that find him selling ice cream to Eskimos, consulting imaginary psychologists and communing with the very first poet—a Neanderthal wordsmith named Sheldon "Big Stones" Firestein.

Matt resides in Cherry Hill, NJ with his wife Ruby, and son, Benny—a beautiful boy who always makes the author smile and laugh with his sheer joy, kindness and playfulness. He endeavors to share his good humor with people, businesses, and organizations while also finding creative ways to help businesses and charities through creative, collaborative gift programs.

For more information on all current, past and future writings and appearances, please visit www.tipofthegoldberg.com, or e-mail matt@tipofthegoldberg.com.